Walking to Ver
A Mostly True Story.

by John J. Dellea IV

DARI GANZAR

T. M.

Walking To Vermont: A Mostly True Story, by John J. Dellea IV

First Edition

DGP Stock Number: PBE 978-0-9854834-6-3

ISBN: 978-0-9854834-6-3

Library of Congress Control Number: 2019913063

Published by:
Dari Ganzar Publishing, LLC
P. O. 441374
Aurora, Colorado 80044-1374

Words are
Magic.

Acknowledgements by John Joseph Dellea, IV

"Once we get out of the eighties, the nineties,
are gonna make the sixties look like the fifties. "
- Huey Walker (Dennis Hopper)
from the 1990 film Flashback

Many of the events depicted and alluded to in this book took place, for the most part, during May of 1992, with the L.A. riots fresh in mind. My mind also made up a lot.

This book, and this alleged Author, owes a debt of gratitude to a whole bunch of people, including, but not limited to:

Cathy, Al, John, Tommy, and Maria. My immediate family, I remember. Always.

My Wife, Catherine L. Mock, who puts up with more than she should. (she is not responsible for my financial debts and obligations.)†

The Dellea Family: too numerous to name.

My Aunts, Madi & Judy.

Various Members of the faculty, staff, and student body of the Vermont College Adult Degree Program, in Montpelier Vermont, who let me mess around with this idea a bit.

Chip & Sue Pancoast for letting me know it is possible to be well adjusted, happy and reasonably normal. And for saving my life at least once.

Jim & Louise Gunderson for showing that it works.

Teri Jirik, whereabouts unknown, for precision.

Betsy Murphy for old times sake.

Ellen Dolan, for what turned out to be early perspective.

Randi Himelgrin & Austin Pfenning, for being bloody improbable.

Dick Hathaway for omelets, a sawbuck, and inspiration.

Rex Burns and Pompa Bannerjee, bandleaders of the C.U. side of the literary chorus in my head.

The Rev. Trygve T. Lode IV, of Denver, Colorado for primitive computer support, chocolate, tolerance, humor, and atheistic inspiration. And cause I promised him I'd put him in the book somewhere.

Katrin Luessenheide, The Synonym Girl, for spellchecking, and being there for the really rough and ugly spots.

The various Saints of the open road: Sam from the South Shore, Stirling from the western slope, Capitola Steve, Mike & Gwenny, A.J. Davis, Rick Dube, Kenny Lewis, Babs & Kesey, and Ray Mungo, wherever the hell you are these days.

Real or imagined inspirational and antagonistic parts have also been played, in varying order, by the following: Edward Abbey, Jack Kerouac, Kurt Vonnegut, Joseph Campbell, Raymond Chandler, T.S. Elliot, National Public Radio, John Jerome, John Irving, Robert B. Parker, Capitol Hill Books in Denver, Spider Robinson, Janet & Stewart Farrar, Carl Jung, John Dunning, Ogden Nash, John Patric, Robert Heinlein, Linus Torvalds, Tom Lehrer, Bill Gates, Ayn Rand, Scott Cunningham, Neal Cassady, Morning Glory & Otter Zell, and the great James Thurber.

The writing of this book also owes a lot to musical doses of J.S. & C.P.E. Bach, Timbuk3, Steve Miller, Led Zeppelin, John Coltrane, The Doors, Charlie Parker, Charles Mingus, The Grateful Dead, Elvis Costello, Djengo Rhinehart, Lou Reed, Peter Himmelman, Neil Young, Ian Anderson, Taj Mahal, Catherine Mock, Clannad, Duane Eddy, Link Wray, Spinal Tap, J. Geils, Bob Dylan, Frank Zappa, David Wilcox, Duke Ellington, The Fools, Dave Brubeck, and W. A. Mozart.

Thanks also to Radio Stations WZLX & WBCN in Boston (Hi, Charles! Hey, Wolf!), KGNU and KBCO in Boulder, and the now defunct KDHT in Denver.

My High School Guidance Counselor, Leonard J. Emmons, who is also of note in that he advised me that "working in a gas station would be better and more realistic" for my development than being a High School Senior. Maybe he was right?

Further thanks (but no blame) for getting this book finally out the door (and enough hope and inspiration and so on) go to fellow "Ink Stained Wretches" Deena Larson and Allen "Big Al" Patterson.

Thanks, I guess, also go to all members of my family and my generous friends, known and unknown, for both positive and negative re-enforcement techniques, love, humor and pain, caffeine, tolerance, sunsets, forests, chocolate, and a deep understanding of some things...

Live Long and Prosper. Be good to each other. Blessed Be!

John J. Dellea, IV
Crow's Nest Cottage,
Boulder County, Colorado, U.S.A.,
October 23, 1994,
November 15, 2002

† Joe and Katherine were subsequently divorced. I'm not certain that if Joe were still alive for this publication, that his rancor at that split would have rescinded enough to include her here. However, I erred on the side of compassion, which is what I know Joe strived to do.

Dedication by the Editor:

Joe signed his will with this for all his friends and relatives. I don't think
he would mind if I left it here also:

Goodbye. I Loved you

And many thanks to John Morse,
for giving me the 2002 version of Joe's book
and to all of Joe's friends who have supported me in this effort.
I thank you all.

Foreword by the Editor

John J. "Joe" Dellea IV was my best friend for nearly twenty years. We met through the Denver Mad Scientists Club and hit it off pretty quickly. We we're both writers, albeit unpublished (except for a few of Joe's early e-zine articles and his pseudonymous Penthouse letters that were published in the late '80s).

Also, we both had a peculiar sense of humor and looking at the world in a way that not too many people share. It is rare to find someone other than your spouse who "gets" you and judges you on your character, not what other people think about you. Joe was that kind of friend.

Joe let me read his road trip memoir from the 1994, <u>Walking to Vermont: A Mostly True Story</u>. I thought it was pretty good. While he was living, our plan was to publish it with Dari Ganzar Publishing, LLC. However, Joe wanted to go through it one more time before he would let me submit it. Unfortunately, he passed away before that could happen.

I say I'm the editor, but to be frank, my role in this was more of the proofreader. I was able to find his 2002 version of his book (thanks again, John Morse) and decided that to honor him and our friendship, I would publish it unedited, except for correcting typos and cutting up long paragraphs into more readable passages. As a result, some of the book may not read as Joe would have liked them. However, if you knew Joe, his true voice is present in his road trip story.

Farewell my friend. You are missed.

A. D. Patterson
August 19, 2019

Chapter 1

On the Road East

"Vladimir and Estragon, Kerouac and Ghengis Khan..."
- Road Song, Loudon Wainwright III

I found my old backpack during the last moving job. I haven't used it since the previous road trip, a couple of years ago.

It's a sort of blue/teal, standard issue student type daypack. Said to be useful for Everest climbs, according to the manufacturer. Padded straps and coup tokens hanging from the zippers.

A lug nut and a nickel with a hole drilled in it dangle from a piece of braided rawhide. A souvenir coin with a rampant dragon from a buddy who worked in the Chinese Government until they weren't watching him and he ran off to be a Baker in Boulder, Colorado. A small ragged feather, and a length of light rope for emergencies. It's been sitting in the hall closet for a while, waiting like a patient dog for its walk.

Hidden in one of the inside pockets is a compass that I promised myself I'd always leave there, a scuffed black Bic lighter that I found on a fencepost near Laramie, and a couple of pens. One of the pens leaked.

I left the bag sitting on the corner of my desk for a couple of days, and somebody asked me about it. "School bag", I'd said.

But I got to thinking about it, and I figured I'd better tell the story to somebody before it doesn't matter anymore. Maybe it already doesn't.

I've got about a week here before the start of my, theoretically, last semester as an undergrad.

What the hell, I've coffee beans in the freezer, and I've got an Atomic brand stove-top espresso machine, from back before they were cool (or self-conscious about power-sources), and a black four cup Braun with a gold filter. I suffered for my art, now it's your turn.

I guess a story should start at the beginning, but with life, those distinctions aren't always so clear. Books are good that way.

In '90 I finally went to college. By '92 I had figured out that I got one that sucked. And that after waiting seven years out of high school. I looked around and found one that looked better, so I signed up. Ten days in Vermont every six months, no problem.

A relationship with a lady that I'd cared about had recently gone kicking and screaming off into the night. Doors had slammed, plates had flown, and, to tell the truth, she had remarkably good aim when she was really moved to it. We'd both said things that were supposed to hurt, and we were supposed to feel like we'd made an amicable parting. That's what she told me anyway.

What it lacked in amiable, it made up for in thorough. I felt like the muffler on a twenty-five dollar car. Yea, trite metaphor, but true nevertheless.

I'd been too emotionally/mentally paralyzed or whatever to really get anything done. No writing, no cooking, no mountains, no walks in the woods. I took final exams a week early at the Bauhaus factory Denver calls a University, and I was on the road.

Ok- maybe that's too much information, or a lousy start. Here, let me try again:

There was a girl I knew back in high school who told me about Diving. Not as a sport, like you see on television, but as a means of going through life.

She said the trick is to tuck your arms up over your ears, keep your feet and knees together tight, and just jump. Keep your form as good as possible and you can fly for a while. The momentum lets you cut through whatever comes up with as little resistance as possible. No time to agonize over it. Too fast to notice. Nothing can stop you because you're just passing through. If you get your trajectory wrong, you miss and it's over before you notice. Oh well.

In her way of seeing it, there is no way a big, professional class, predator can come for you, as long as you're In Motion. You're moving fast, and nothing matters but the motion. You just jump: you don't have to think or kick your feet, the sharks can't see you, and you're long gone before they even know you've been there.

Her boyfriend accidentally got them both killed just after Graduation. Took a guardrail in a '69 Camaro at something over a hundred. It took two days to dredge enough of the muddy Merrimac River to find them.

I guess my story starts at a point of departure too.

My roommate Maryanne gave me a ride out to the truck stop at the far edge of Denver. She said that if she could have afforded it, she would have driven me to the Nebraska border, some two hundred miles away. We'd been lovers once.

I left New England at age twenty one, during the manic 80's to try and find what the 70's hippies found in the West. Boulder, Colorado. Dan Fogelberg, Caribou Studios, Celestial Seasonings, Rocky Mountain Highs, Mork From Ork. All that good shit.
I fled all the way from Boston's 128 to central Cow Hampshire before the tide of the Yuppie Diaspora of the mid 80's. Call it a practice run. Ostensibly, I'd been chasing a girl then too, but that wasn't the important part; at least it didn't turn out to be.

I ended up homeless in Boulder's hottest Summer, and lived in my car up in the canyons for a while, trying to survive, and figure out what else was important. I did some carpentry, read some old books, hocked some personal possessions, and I thought a lot. Took over a year to get back indoors full time.

Anyway, when Maryanne dropped me off at the exit ramp in front of the Tomahawk Truck Stop, it took me almost fifteen minutes to get out of the car and cross the exit ramp.

Yes, I'll be careful. No candy from strangers, absolutely not. Yes, I'll call. Yes, I'll look both ways when I cross the street. Yes, I'll be back, I promise....

We'd stopped for cigarettes at a 7-11 on the way out of town. Generic Light 100's. I realized, as soon as I reached the other side of the road, that I'd left one of the two packs on the seat of her old Pontiac. Hidden, no doubt, by an empty Diet Pepsi bottle, tissues, make-up, a couple of fast food bags and a very used looking hairbrush. In that morass of candy wrappers, Slurpee cups, and feminine beauty items, they may never surface. (note: to the best of my knowledge they haven't yet.)

I once saw, in a truck stop in Chicago, a poster that showed a piece of sinfully rich looking chocolate cake and a can of diet soda; the caption read "EAT AMERICAN". Maryanne lives on that principal, and it hasn't let her down yet.

Forgetting your spare pack of cigarettes at the beginning of a trip like this is not what you might call a good omen.

At noon it was about eighty-five degrees and kind of hazy, which was a bit early, for the first week of May in Colorado. I guess I was glad to be going, because I had been into a rut, stagnation state, for a long time.

Once it doesn't matter anymore, it's easy.

Sometimes it takes dynamite to get you off the couch; travel often helps. Adventure. Travel. Go to foreign lands, meet exciting and interesting people, exploit and kill them.

Whoops, sorry, that's the Military Industrial Complex. Wrong decade. Wrong book, probably.

I just wanted to see some things, and get the job done. Because I had to do something. Something to do. Nothing like a bit travel to clear the cobwebs and give you some perspective. Don't think, accelerate.

At twenty-four I enrolled in college. I guess to find a clean way to make a living. The prospect of career opportunities that involved saying "You want fries with that?" was somewhat, uh, unexciting.

So I walked into the information office at the local college and said, " I want to go to school. What do I do?"

Never miss an opportunity to be straightforward. It scares the hell out of people, amuses those with a sense of irony and gives the simpler folk an explanation for why you're in front of them.

I'm large, so-called Caucasian, poor, and my Grade Point Average sucks. This does not put me high on scholarship lists, so they gave me to their Denver satellite campus.

Denver has its drawbacks, like the regular smell of Dog Chow from the big Purina plant on the North side of the city, and a "Brown Cloud" that made the place seem to be ensconced in a filthy Fuller Dome.

But I worked it out: by mortgaging the future with Financial Aid, I could afford a studio apartment and regular food. After two years, I had a chance to go to school in Vermont, a big green place with a reputation for sweetness.

The problem was that I had to find a way to get there for two weeks every six months. Funny bureaucratic glitch; schools will only give you the money if you are physically present. Sometimes not even then. Study is assumed.

I'd grown up in a straight working class Boston-Irish family and gone to a high school that didn't figure that you really mattered unless you were going directly to college after they were done with you. It didn't matter what for, as long as you were going.

At eighteen I had no idea where the hell I fit into the world and was afraid I'd make some decision that I'd later regret. So, naturally, I became a mechanic for a couple of years: grease is great protective coloration. I worked as a parts man for an auto-parts place for a while, then I worked for the Internal Revenue Service for a bit: Cleanliness and money are even better.

I had ten bucks in my pocket and a week to get there. I wrote to my Dad, told him I was coming home, and asked him to scout around for a cheap set of wheels for the return trip. American pickup or van of a vintage that could be repaired rather than have defective units replaced by guys in lab coats.

"You want Fries with that?"

Walk, or practice that phrase. Anything in pursuit of the holy College Degree. The 80's proved that a college degree is the bare minimum to get out of minimum wage. Knowledge is power and power requires struggle ("By any means necessary").

Besides, there is "The Road", a sacrament, a rite of passage. It's about the only one still in reach these days, alliterated and alluded to in most of the best tales of humanity. Buddha, Saul of Tarsus, King Arthur, Jack Kerouac, Tolkien, Deadheads, and The Fuller Brush Man are all members of that sacred fraternity of the long and winding metaphor. Hit the road Jack.

I reached the white line at the edge of the road and looked back towards the brown cloud that covers the city like a nicotine stained contact lens, and I could just make out Maryanne's car receding in the distance, doing it's part to help out. I walked back onto the little triangular patch of grass and weeds that form geometric islands between exit ramps and the highway the world over, and sat down on a small anthill. The ants were not happy. Just what I get for taking the formal approach. Sitting meditation is over-rated.

I got up and dusted myself off and thought about Jack Kerouac and whether or not he started out like this. I read him when I was thirteen or so, and he sure seemed to have a lot more fun in those seemingly innocent days. Old Jack, that crazy Zen Buddhist Cannuck from my homeland of North Eastern Industrial Massachusetts, lived in a much more gentle time.

Bob Dylan said, to the generation between Jack's, and mine "to live outside the law you must be honest". It takes much more energy to live on the edge than to build the security to live comfortably. But it has a kind of integrity. It has mythological Power, even if only for yourself.

Thinking for yourself is hard work, and fitting in can be a kind of slow death.

I can't say, for example, that I'm always honest; I see it, for example, as a duty to lie to any institution that is more interested in my identification numbers and little plastic cards than with who I am. I'm as honest as I can manage to be with People; it seems important. It took me a long time to figure it out, and I'm still not always sure, but, from this story, that much will probably be evident. This is, I'm told, a defiant stance. So be it. At least I haven't had to dye my hair blue or get an earring like the rest of the rebels.

I picked a better location and sat down to do a last minute check of all "my gear." It really didn't consist of much.

Two bags and the prerequisite scruffy and faded denim jacket. The larger bag, a daypack suitable for carrying schoolbooks up mountains (according to the manufacturers), contained my extra pair of jeans, five pair of socks, two plastic bags, half a roll of toilet paper and three spare shirts. The other pack, a rectangular Korean war surplus gas mask bag, contained floppy disks for my home-built PC, all the bullshit paperwork that I thought I might need at school, as well as two knives and a pound of granola supplemented with cashews and chocolate chips.

I don't know about the granola, but I'm fairly sure that Jack Kerouac never carried floppy disks. I think the name would have made him grin.

Somebody told me that I'm a member of a thing called "Generation X", and I'm supposed to be confused by all this cultural context stuff. That helps a hell of a lot. If I'm a member, do I get a card? If I get a card, will it be my duty to befuddle everybody my own age with obscure pop-culture references? Why? A certain beer company uses an ad slogan "Why ask Why?": the answer to that should be self evident.

Yea, I was a kid in the seventies, and got stuck with all the stupid experiments they could come up with, ranging from "New Math" and leisure suits to Koogle brand chocolate peanut butter spread food, Pong, television reruns of Gilligan's Island and Hogan's Heroes (I wonder what B'nai B'rith's attitude is on this?) to the friends' parents who signed up for EST and wouldn't let the kids go to the bathroom. I know of one couple who taught their kid the colors wrong, just to see what would happen. Screw the Golden Age of the Baby Boom.

Myths come from a box with an antenna. The Baby Boomer's first nostalgia craze was Happy Days, a TV show about how good it was to be clean cut in the Eisenhower Years, was the big deal when I was in grade school. The word AIDS was coined around the time I was fifteen, and the "freedom fighters of the sexual revolution" had sounded retreat after leaving around enough propaganda for me to guess at the loss. I know three people who don't come from "Broken Homes", this gives me membership in something? Show me an ID card.

I don't have any friends as nervy as Neal Cassady, and they've turned his beloved Larimer Street into a Yuppie-Mall-Thing, complete with bottled water and three dollar-a-cup coffee, anyway. A thing called "Writer's Square" that certainly wouldn't welcome them now.

"Oh, glorious Denver, Queen City of the plains...".

Steinbeck did his last cross-country jaunt with rare books, reams of paper, bottles of good brandy and a dog. (Not to mention seemingly unlimited funds and a camper bigger than my apartment.) Way out of my league, but still part of the trip. "We don't take a trip," said Steinbeck, "The trip takes us." The Road is a continuum.

I was born in the small-scale closeness of Boston's nearly respectable industrial northern suburbs, where the distant highway flowed like the rivers of Huck Finn's youth. The constant rippling burble of the road was so far in the background that only a few could hear. I guess I did, and one day I left.

Right? Ain't that the point?

I ate some granola, took a drink from my canteen (Vietnam surplus) and smoked a cigarette. Smoking cigarettes and eating granola is one of those dichotomies that I have decided to just live with.

7

In Boulder, tobacco use is sort of frowned on as unhealthy and probably a sub-yuppie proletariat activity, and not in a good way. If you can't afford them, it's bourgeois. If you can, it's unenlightened.

Kerouac is a local patron saint, and he smoked. But then again, he never actually got to Boulder. If you smoke there, it's supposed to be one of those organic brands or an exotic import. I grew up with some very opposite messages and I've tried to find a rational middle ground.

I know I should give up the smoking, it's bad for me, but I've rarely ever had three days to book off for psychosis. Refer to me as a "slacker", and maybe I'll quit just before I come over to your house.

Look, the country is beautiful and diverse, you can learn a lot from the people you meet, but the objective sometimes, to keep it in context, is to get from one place to the other, in one piece, as quickly as possible. Travel. Dive through.

The most valuable life learning can come from contact with other people. The next best to life learning is that from books or direct experience. Almost anything you could want to know is in a book somewhere. Most people just watch the television.

When your objective is flat speed rush travel, you are just trying to eliminate distance. Screw the subtleties of learning from modes of living, dynamite the Midwest and push the fucking coasts together. E=mc2. Speed, visceral, real, speed of motion, not the chemical shit, is the drug. Maybe it's the ultimate drug.

Cassady's gone ghost chants: "Go Go Go Man Go Go Go Go!"

I sat in the American version of the lotus position, watching the ants. I had another smoke while I thought about this, and asked myself 'why I was really doing this?'

It's American Lotus because I've got short thick legs, and as an American there used to be a divine right to pervert anything we want. God said it was OK. Ask John Wayne.

The thoughts percolated like a boiling mantra. Speed. Speed. Speed. Why Am I doing this?

The answer, of course, is simple: I'm an idiot. Going to a school on the other side of the country, when your annual income is less than most people pay for car insurance, is just plain silly. Going to college is important, and unless you can really hustle, it's virtually impossible to get to do anything interesting without education exemplified on vellum.

It would have been nice to be born rich; I'm planning on it next time around, (well, that or cute) but look at all the fun I would have missed. When I lived up in the canyon, I had to worry about the deer eating my lunch before I did. That just don't happen in the 'burb's.

There is an old Chinese curse that says "may you live in interesting times." It didn't sound like a curse the first time I heard it, but it is one of those things that can sneak up on you. Zen sneaky.

There had been riots in Los Angeles the previous week and all the "rob the poor and give to the rich" tactics of twelve years of Republican leadership had paid off. The ghettos were burning. Yuppies were crash robbing computer stores with their highly insured Beemers and later calling their insurance agents on their cell-phones to report they'd been car-jacked.

Only a couple of years to go until the millennial clock ticks another eon. The Fundamentalists always think that whatever god it is that they favor likes round numbers, so, according to history, it is likely to get weirder out. Last millennium it got weird out for a couple of hundred years.

Massachusetts, New Hampshire, and Colorado: hoping to hitchhike to Vermont. The sixties were over, right? No more peaceful folk around. Yuppie lawyers on crack and steroids, who'll swear on their credit rating that they were at Woodstock (the first one).

Free love? It's a stupid cliché anyway. Ain't no such thing as a free lunch, never-mind love. No way, no how. But this is the myth of my childhood. Be peaceful, and loving, and it will all come to you.

I don't know if I buy it, but one of these days I've got to learn how to play the guitar.

Chapter 2

Coldfacts Avenue, Denver, Summer Before

"God sometimes you just don't come through..."
-Tori Amos

The driver clears his throat over the speaker on the number 15 bus in a way that sounds like he's dislodging a hairball.

He's an old black man, wrinkled and shrunken, and he usually tells lousy jokes that he laughs at himself. Sometimes you can't help but laugh along. He has a good smile and sharp eyes. If you come out of nowhere running for the bus, he'll see you and stop. He's my favorite bus-driver.

It's 9:10 in the morning and it's already 89 degrees according to the light-up sign on the bank.

The bus is packed to the bursting point with the people of the East Colfax neighborhood, a dry-rot conglomeration of mansions turned into cramped apartments with scarred heavy paint. What people from West of Chicago mean when they say slum.

It's turning Yuppie now. Gentrification, or whatever the hell it is. The rents along here have doubled in the last three years, and will probably double again after that. And you can feel the pressure building.

The narrow line of backbeat tension is growing a little tighter, every day. The ordinary day-to-day rip-offs are even getting mean lately. This is where the poor people go, the ones who never got it quite right, and it's sort of a tradition that it's like this since the "nice people" abandoned the city for the 'burbs, a generation back.

It's ugly, and more confusing lately. Van Gogh said, about The Night Cafe, that it was " A place you could lose your soul". Vinnie never saw a Fern Bar gentrify his neighborhood to death.

The Driver clears his throat over the mike again like a pot scrubber in a garbage disposal, "I heard it's gonna be a hun-nerd an' ten t'day..."

He's as apologetic as battlefield comfort.

The people are silent. It's ninety now, and the day just started. Life sucks sometimes, and there is just some shit you have got to put up with. Most of these folks don't have air conditioning, or even a fan. If they do, it costs them a serious portion of their income. Most don't. Resignation and not a word. "Cool" is a word, and it has frosty beer sign icicles hanging from it.

"...Down in Ari-zona", he said after the regulation ten seconds. "I'd believe it about that place."

The hammer just dropped on an empty chamber.

His laugh sounds like a dog's squeak-toy.

A little laughter and some uneasy chuckling.

Awkward grins, and unaccustomed real, but tenuous laughter. A wave of ease starts to move.

An odd sound. A thin woman with a pierced nose, and at least six earrings per side, in black from her boots to her dye-job, laughs in series' of five-chuckle staccato bursts. It's a flat sound, almost mechanical. Like a musical wind-up toy with a bad gear.

If you know that sound, it doesn't matter what you're wearing.

The smiles sort of freeze in place, as the rest of the laughter stops. Maybe we all know that sound in ourselves from somewhere.

A fat Mexican lady in an intricate kerchief crosses herself as we pass the Cathedral of The Immaculate Conception, her lips moving fast and silently.

The laugh continues.

There's not going to be any release until we get to Broadway.

A muscular white guy, in jeans, T-shirt, and laborer's dirt over his tattoos, takes off his hat, ("Newport, Alive with Pleasure!") and runs his fingers through his thin long hair. A couple, with Down's Syndrome, hold hands and lean together, the shoulders of their wine colored Fast-food uniforms touching each other solidly. A balding man in a cheap light blue suit lets go of the overhead bar to adjust his tie and is knocked off balance, but cannot fall because we're packed in so tight.

The Laugh Continues.

Two Japanese tourist girls, in white summer blouses and trim blue shorts, keep their faces blank, but their hands flutter near their small daypacks like magicians handkerchiefs about to produce doves. A skinny guy, in a straw cowboy hat, frayed at the brim, reaches a neat index finger inside his fastened top shirt button to make room for his shuttling Adam's Apple. A fat white guy, who told this tale, checks the eyes he can see. A pretty redheaded secretarial type tries to act like nothing is amiss. A hardcore Gangsta Rap guy, so cool he's wearing a black wool hat, tries to stare her down from over his Ray-Ban's. A Sergio Leone moment.

And the Goddamned Laugh just keeps going on...

It's eight blocks to Broadway, and it looks like some of us are going to have The Laugh on the edge of our minds all day. At least it will pass, we hope. The bus is going Downtown.

Where do you think you go when you go off the edge?

Chapter 3

Dharma Surfing

"...the last American Hero, to whom speed is the freedom of the soul.
And the question is not when he's going to stop,
but who is going to stop him."
- Super Soul (Cleavon Little), in Vanishing Point (1971 film)

"We are a culture desperately in need of myths and rituals."
- Joseph Campbell

"Beauty is in the eye of the storm."
- Graffiti, Muddy's Java Cafe, Denver, 1993

I walked across the road and stuck out one of the signs that Maryanne had made for me. It's a hell of a good sign. I've still got it, sitting in the chair with the backpack across the room as I write this. Done in heavy magic marker on some kind of faced white art paper a quarter of an inch thick; folded in half it reads "Vermont" (with a peace symbol in the letter "O", of course), on one side and "East" on the other. Next to the word "East" is the cartoon character Opus from the strip "Bloom County"; he is sticking out his left thumb and is wearing a T-shirt that reads "NORWICH UNIVERSITY, VERMONT, no walruses please".

The shoes were fairly new, and I had to get the balance and the old swivel on the ball of the right foot down right again. One, two, three, turn. One, two, three, turn. Long out of practice. I hiked Northwest on I-76 out of the Denver brown cloud for about an hour, just to get a walking pace, sizing up the cars, thinking about the process, eliminating expectations, and putting up the psychic defenses before being picked up by a kid in a truly battered black and yellow Plymouth Barracuda.

The thing was a masterpiece of the late teens do it yourself school of transportation creation. No fender undented, no electrical connection un-mickey-moused. Rust in some eventually terminal places.

P.J. O'Rourke talks about this as an archetype: acne and a leather jacket; wide balding tires with three lug nuts on each rust-spotted chrome wheel. An extremely rare thing in these times of bi-annual vehicle inspections and such. A well broken-in example of a theoretically better, vanished, age. It looked a lot like the Chevelle I drove in High School.

Imagine what it's like to be eighteen or twenty, with a fast car of your own, in the midst of a world that looks like wide open space. On a smooth road, your own music way up loud, and nothing to worry about when you're out on the road, away from the rest of your life. It's *sooo* good the first time.

He only got me about twenty miles along, but it really helped my perspective when he noticed that the time on my watch corresponded with the cubic inches of his motor. Whatever works. An irrelevant omen perhaps, but the 318 was good motor in its day and it's a fine time of the afternoon. It probably even works out to be numerologically lucky or something.

Good and bad omens are everywhere if you've just the eyes to see. Adjust the eyes to see. Only a fool fails to hear a proffered bit of hope or insight when it's needed. Like that joke where God says "Hey, I sent you two boats and a helicopter, what more do you want?" Any hope will do sometimes.

I always did wonder about the magical and metaphysical implications of that Chrysler Pentastar emblem.

He said what I was doing was cool, and he wished we could trade places. I didn't say anything about that until now, but I'm grinning. Told him that what he was doing was pretty cool, too, but he said he was "just riding around".

The next ride served to re-affirm the positive feelings. The vibe was going smooth. I'd just gotten down to the bottom of the exit ramp and was almost immediately picked up by a fellow who was dressed in civil war garb, tooling along in a Japanese minivan. Seems normal enough to me.

Jeans, a Confederate tunic and a Yankee cavalry hat. He was drinking a Diet Pepsi and wearing John Lennon glasses: I guess I have a weird sense about who is "okay", but, as a guideline, when you see somebody that involved in something like historical recreation, you can guess that their main involvement is something other than going around hurting people. He too was only going about thirty miles but was willing to tell me about himself and what he was into.

He was a sometimes street musician and periodic History Teacher. All the hardware (including flags and cannon parts on the back floor) was for the battles that he recreated and staged with and for grade school kids. He showed me an article, paper-weighted by an imitation Navy Colt service revolver that I had failed to notice, from the last week's Greeley Tribune. It showed a bunch of kids in authentic looking civil war uniforms trying to take a hill. It told about the amount of planning and the degree of accuracy, and the value of the experience. I hadn't thought that you could interest kids in anything that didn't come with an electrical cord. No Nintendo, No deal man.

He told me how much the kids got into it, and about the work that he and his family put into getting the costumes ready. He spent weekends prowling thrift shops for appropriate clothes, and his mother and girlfriend put in a lot of time altering them. The details were correct right down to the buttons to fit the period and the rank. Hell, he had a guy who made pewter buttons by the pound.

In the towns that he had done it, everybody had turned out to watch, help out and participate. Someday, he said, he might break even, but it was a good time. It made me feel good to know that somebody was able to do that kind of thing for kids.

I went to grade school in the early seventies and had the good fortune to get many of the teachers who went to college to avoid the Vietnam draft. As a child then, the news was my bedtime story. Martin Luther King, Bobby Kennedy, The March on Washington. Resurrection City was someplace I heard about along side of New York, Jerusalem, Dublin, and Hanoi.

"The sixties", whatever the hell that means, were the highest widest time in our culture's history. Its Protest Songs were the nursery rhymes of my childhood. Kid's don't know that it is unusual for rabbits to be in magician's hats, or for police to drag handcuffed people around by the ankles. I grew up thinking that the day's body count from the war was supposed to come just before the sports scores. That was just what I saw.

The saints of the time were just part of the pantheon. Jack & Bobby Kennedy, Dr. King, Jesus, Jimi Hendrix, Abe Lincoln, Janis Joplin, The Beatles: these were who you looked up to. These were who you

15

prayed to when you saluted the flag, or put your head on your desk for the school prayer, or when you curled up under your desk during the air raid drills. This was who you prayed to, so that everything would be okay.

Some of those schoolteachers were, if they were young enough, some of the finest and most creative teachers I have ever heard of. When many of them turned to an interest in their careers and making money around the time I hit junior high, the educational system in this country suffered a great deal. This fellow was a representative of what I had thought to be an extinct species.

He dropped me off in one of those sagebrush Colorado towns that is not much more than a freeway exit with a gas station and a grain elevator. I was feeling pretty good about the world as a whole.

As said, the Los Angeles Riots had been the week before and I was not sure what the general mood in the country was. The twelve year long Republican field day was in its last months, and I hoped that change was imminent. I was hoping for a return of the peaceful hippie, or even the Great Depression spirit of cooperation. All the corporate loot and burn raiding had a hundred thousand people a week filing for unemployment and ten percent of the population was on food stamps. Maybe the current mania for "Family Values", as espoused by the Republicans, was supposed to be accomplished when people were forced to band together to survive by hunting the rich.

When the bread and circus amusements of seventy cable channels and color televisions with built in video tape machines wore thin, when the people had too little food and failed to be distracted by their bright toys, I was afraid that it would get really ugly out. Afraid the worst aspects of the sixties were returning with a frenetic crack cocaine fueled vengeance.

I really did not know what to expect out there on the road and was pretty nervous about the whole thing. It's considered dumb, or at least naive to say "I love my country". I do, or, more specifically, I love its people and places and the basic ideas behind its founding.

The idea of a whole city reduced to burning rubble scared the hell out of me. Los Angeles is a golden city of the West. Spoken of in hushed and reverent or hopeful tones from Paris and Tokyo to the diminishing Rainforest and the blossoming desert cities of the Middle East. That much anger and frustration just below the surface is a scary thing. Even the tamest of people is only a week's food away from homicide, and it's hard to look at all our technological advances and remember that. Reality can be brutally harsh.

Stone axes, silicon chips and spray can cave paintings of BMW's in the alleys of the 'hood.

I am now positive that I read altogether too much Plato, Emerson and Thoreau as a teenager. That innocent idealism of a supposedly simpler time. I read all that stuff as a child, and a few people encouraged me because it was supposed to be good, solid literature, and a lot of people who nod sagely and grunt approval have only reputations and rumors to go on.

Big Secret: These people were considered menaces to their own societies. Reprehensible miscreants who corrupt the minds of the youth and such. And there never were simpler times.

Maybe my idealism began to crack when I went to Walden Pond to commune with the spirit of Little Henry's project. Even signed the petition to keep a goddamned condo developer away from the place. I thought that I too would like to move out to the woods and live simply, I still do. A solar panel mountain cabin with one room devoted entirely to floor to ceiling bookshelves with a rolling ladder on a track: a Franklin Stove, canning jars in the pantry, and a fast computer. Maybe a four-car garage and a machine shop out back. I'm willing to build it myself.

It can't be done Thoreau's way. Laborers, observed Ms. Woolf to a bunch of bright young men at an expensive college, don't have the luxury of time for deep thought and study. Farmers have a hell of a time being Yeomen.

Sure, Henry had some nice ideas, but when I was there I stood where the cabin had been. It was accidentally burned down by "tramps" during the Thirties, but you can still tell the place, you can feel the vibe, so sacred to Idealists and Dreamers the world over. I heard, off through the woods, the sound of a guided tour going on at Emerson's house.

Little Henry, it seems, had been camped out in his friend Ralph's back yard like a kid in a tent with a flashlight and a pile of comic books. But he meant well.

A couple of years later, I was in a bar in southern New Hampshire, and saw Thoreau's Mother's washing machine. Technically and mechanically interesting and bringing home the idea that the hearty nineteenth century adventurer might have been just a bit of a fraud. Idealist: Accent on the prefix. But history belongs to the person telling the story, and Henry meant well, and he did make his own pencils.

I was so high on my good fortune, and the fast pace of the rides so far, that I went into town and bought a celebratory soda and a package of cheese crackers, and ate them sitting on the edge of the highway (and sat down on the edge of a prickly pear cactus- they have pretty yellow flowers, but they hurt like hell!). Trying to feel thoughtful and meditative in spite of the fact that the trip was gaining ground rapidly. When you sit in the desert, watch your ass. Dharma surfing on the breakdown lane. Who told the food manufacturers that cheese is bright orange?

I walked for a while and was almost immediately picked up by a fellow who was an out-of-work miner. Said he'd failed the medical over something that might or might not get better. He was from Leadville, a mountain town which consists of some houses in unlikely places and more bars per person than any other place on earth.- so sayeth Guinness' little record book. He had all of his possessions in a rusty old Wagoneer, and was going home to be with relatives. Said he missed them pretty hard.

They would let him sleep in his truck out in the yard and that would be enough to get him through this particular hard-time. Then he'd go back, he said. His kids had been staying with his wife's family since she had died.

He was in rough shape. He told me of how tough the times were in the hill country. How the good, honest, mountain folks were being pushed out by the "yuckies" (yuppies).

It seems that "some strange new kind of damned hippies called "environmeddlers", the E.P.A., bankers in neckties and all manner of other incomprehensible folks had been turning up around there lately. They made like working with your hands and getting dirty was something nasty. Shit, not everybody can live like them people on the television. You order a beer in a bar, you pay for it and you finish it."

We talked about Carpentry, which is what I do when I need a real job, and Mining, which was what he did since he was fourteen. Said that he admired the fact that I was going to school, and he allowed as how he had thought about doing that himself as a way to get more unemployment money and maybe a better job and such, but the people who are in charge of the paperwork were pretty unreasonable folks, telling a man he ain't fit to learn stuff, 'cause he don't turn in papers right away.

Although he was working on something closer to Navajo time, which acknowledges few time units shorter than a season, I could see his point, Paperwork vs. Life. He'd been invaded and put out of work by television characters without fingerprints. His hands looked like scuffed baseball mitts with calluses, and grey stone dust worked deeply into them.

How and when did the world get so confusing?

"What the hell is wrong with being a workingman?" he asked me.

I'd seen the times change incomprehensibly on my father and grandfather, Old School Truckmen; my great-grandfather was in the freight business with a horse. They used to make multiple copies of lading bills by hand.

I didn't know what to tell him. In the business now are guys who don't know how the trucks work: Guys who wear polyester uniforms just like you get if you work fast-food. Freight Biz-ness, you want fries with that?

You can tell a lot about a person by their hands. I've met five foot tall female Jewelers who could bend a penny between their fingers, and Construction foremen who get nasty paper-cuts.

He dropped me off at his exit and wished me well. We shook hands like climbers, and his old Jeep rattled down the ramp through the dust.

Off to the side of I-76, somewhere near where he dropped me, in the more or less former town of Ovid, Colorado, there used to be a gas station. It is the only thing you can see from the highway except grass and sky and the highway.

The gutted remains of the place sit there among the tan grassy hills, abandoned and remote. Lying on the broken tar of the pump island, amid the chamomile, prickly pear and buffalo grass, strewn with black tar rocks and bright greenish crystals of safety glass, there is a rusted orange and white circular sign for a brand of fuel I don't remember. Weeds grow out of the cracks in the paving and from between the cracks in the cinderblock walls. They hadn't even finished boarding it up.

Ovid. Greatest poet of ancient Greece. Said to have written the book of love. Someone had high hopes here once. The starkness of the land, out here on the high plains, can gobble your dreams.

Chapter 4

"Indians"

"No experiment can be more interesting than that we are now trying, and which we trust will end in establishing the fact that man may be governed by reason and truth."
-Thomas Jefferson

"Whoever sets himself up to be a judge of truth and knowledge is shipwrecked by the laughter of the gods."
-Albert Einstein

I have to admit that I wimped out on my first winter in Colorado.

I had been living there for about eight months, working and getting my life together after a significant number of mistakes. It was November; winter was coming on and I had nothing to fall back on when carpentry work dried up for the season.

A friend back home said I could get some temporary warehouse work on the graveyard shift that might, at least last the winter. Use one of the back bedrooms at his place.

I decided to go "home" for the winter and give that life another try. I packed all of my stuff back into my dying car and headed out for where Home used to be.

I guess the initial Idea for this book came out of that trip. I realized that I'd spent a lot of time in my life with people talking, and had heard a lot of them without *really* Listening. When I began to try to really hear what people had to say, it was *surprising*.

I was not more than fifty miles outside of Denver when I stopped to help out a man and woman whose truck, an International Harvester Scout, had broken down. They had to get home to be with a sick relative. It was getting on toward night, and to make a long story short, it was agreed that I would give them a ride as far in their direction as I was going.

James and Barbara. "Indian" is the common word I grew up on to describe them. He said he liked the term "Indigenous Peoples", but it was hard to get that one to stick. She said "People", which was, in fact, the Oglala Word for themselves. I never heard the word Oglala before I came to the West.

We talked about where we were from. We fell to the discussion of how our two cultures had met, and the net results.

As they told me about the rampant alcoholism on their reservation, the bad housing and way-the-hell-below poverty line conditions that the noble Oglala people were now subject to, I was ashamed. I've since been to a couple of Reservations. I am ashamed of what my country has done to these people.

I'm a "white man", in the common usage of those terms; male, Caucasian, with Irish and Italian roots. Maybe a little Brit thrown in, way in the hell back. I know my family line, and, as these things go, my ancestors come out pretty clean. Too busy being oppressed minorities themselves to be screwing people over, but I don't know as that makes a hell of a lot of difference.

As a student of history, I knew how they had been cheated and mistreated. Smallpox blankets, Sand Creek, Buffaloes killed for a pound of tongue meat.

The question is, of course, why?

I began to search my mind for a reason why these people had been so exploited. Who the hell were they hurting? What was their "sin"? Which seems to be a justification for taking the other guy's stuff in previous centuries.

In looking at the history of this, my culture, it is evident that not any one group had been going around subverting cultural and spiritual wealth. Worldwide, it is easy to say that the villain is The Church, British Colonialism, Spanish Colonialism, French Colonialism, Yankee Imperialism, Capitalism, Socialism, Maoist Reductionism or any of a number of individual conquerors that caused the greatest damage to indigenous cultures.

These are all precursors to "uncaring bureaucracy"- by the time that sets in, you're screwed.

The victor is the most creative killer. The American Cavalry invented what has become known as the "Concentration Camp" (yes, Hitler *did* steal the idea).

Because two leaders disagree on a subject, say Economics, Land, or Religion, people die. Thousands, sometimes *MILLIONS* of people die because of the failure of their leaders to understand a people or country that "the people" may have no argument with.

The Boxer Mohammed Ali went to jail for two years for refusing to go to Vietnam. His reason, he said, was that no Vietcong had ever insulted him and he had suffered worse insult at the hands of his own countrymen.

The real problem I think is the tradition of war and the desire to beat people up to convert them to the predominant (The victor's) mode of thought. That's one hell of a bad habit. After all, isn't God on the side of the victor?

I told them this and that I felt that "modern" culture had been getting better at this as time went on. Europeans, after all, had learned it from Rome, both versions. They had all been making the world safe for Christianity for so long that they had no instinctual respect left for anybody who was not of whatever "One True Faith" was in charge at the time.

When North America was "discovered" all of Europe had a "new" group to work out their aggressions on, enslave, exploit, convert to Christianity or kill as necessary. Sometimes all of the above. And they could send the most brutal and stupid among them someplace else, while telling them that they are brave. Watch for this trend if Space colonization ever gets going on a real level. There are rarely good table manners on a frontier for a reason.

We talked about the way the native peoples of this land had offered their soon to be bitten open hand. How they had laughed at the idea of owning land.

We talked about similarities and dissimilarities of our faiths, or philosophies of life (I am a Pagan, which, for me, is a sort of attempt to get back to the spirituality of my pre-Christian Celtic ancestors.) and stuff like that. For example, most Pagans are matrifocal or dualistic, The Oglala are Patrifocal. We're both fairly Animistic. I'm sort of a devout

Academic Polytheist with Taoist Buddhist leanings- they weren't. And how that was okay. We were both trying to get to the same place for the same reasons.

The man told me that I shouldn't be upset about how humans treat each other. He said struggle creates strength.

We sat in my car outside of a McDonald's in North Platte Nebraska and he told me that the Creator of the Universe had made two mistakes:

Giving humans different languages and skin colors was the first: Because if people cannot talk to each other they cannot understand each other.

The second was giving them pockets: If you have pockets, you want to put things in them. If you begin to accumulate things then sooner or later you get greedy.

A New Age Christian friend of mine says that the last is opposite to "walking in the Garden"; a state where "God provides". Contrary to the main ideals of the nineteen eighties James Watt trip. Mr. Watt once said that it was "not necessary to preserve natural resources, because "The Rupture" would be happening soon". He was in charge of the U.S. Department of the Interior at the time.

We had talked. We learned from each other. We learned about each other, and are not strangers anymore. I haven't seen them since. I left that restaurant parking lot with their words rattling around in my brain.

I take the words out and think about them from time to time. I try to think about our inhabitation of the planet as a stewardship. Even if we do own this planet in the sense that King James' Bible gives us, don't you think our "Heavenly Father" will be upset if we don't take good care of our things?

I'd given James and Barbara a loaf of the corn bread that I'd made for the trip, in a friend's kitchen in Boulder and they'd bought me a cup of coffee. Their friends would be down to meet them and bring them home. If I hurried, I too could be home in time for Thanksgiving, they said. The irony didn't hit me until much later.

Humans are all the same. Moslem, Christian, Jew, Hindu, Pagan, Buddhist, Atheist or Zoroastrian, black, white, red, brown, yellow, or green, the biological difference is less than .0000001%. All the rest is difference of opinion.

The only way to stop fearing strangers is for them to stop being strangers. This is one of the only truths I know.

Chapter 5

The Art of Truckin'

"The woods are long and dark and deep,
and I have miles to go before I sleep.
-Robert Frost, American Poet

I started walking again, and put on another hour or so before a tractor-trailer stopped for me just outside the town of Hillrose. The Driver told me his name was Brad and I told him mine. He said that he was way too tired, but had to make it home tonight. Simple human companionship can keep you alive out here.

He told me some stories of the road, and the different loads that he's had and what a fool his Dispatcher is. Ask any Trucker: The Dispatcher is always either evil or incompetent. Most of the ones I've met really are as nasty and corrupt as that little guy on the TV show Taxi.

Some dispatchers are a separate species specifically designed to hustle people into doing things they don't want to do. Like being away from home. It's what they do for a living.

Exceptions are rare and have hearts of purest gold. Most try to let you believe they're doing you a favor. Somehow they always want to dress as Pimps for Halloween.

Brad and I talked about the riots and the different attitudes that we had both encountered around the country. We swapped a few trucking stories. He had been driving for fifteen years, and my Dad has been driving a truck, off and on, for about thirty, and my grandfather for more than that. So I knew a few tales too.

A Roadie folk-legend, that is adapted to whatever the locale: It seems that there was this speed trap, and a particular state trooper had it in for a particular small group of drivers; truckers. Had a perfect hideout for the trap.

One of the drivers knows an electronics wizard. A fishing boat Loran system is modified and mounted in the air conditioner box on top of the tractor and the truckers go out hunting "Bear". When the radar detector on the dash goes off, the switch on the Loran is activated and sends back a signal in the same frequency as the radar gun, but several hundred times more powerful.

Smoke and cops pour out of the cruiser windows as the truckers go rolling by. It's a quirk of the setup on police cars that use hand radar guns that the cop will often keep the actual radar gun in their lap.

There is a variation that involves frustrated guys on an Air Force Base and an AWACS jamming module.

We were well over the Nebraska State Line before either of us stopped laughing, or ran out of tall tales about the three strangest and most inexplicable animals on the road: People in cars, Rookie Truck Drivers and Cops. All of which can do some pretty funny things.

He showed me pictures, Velcroed to the dash, of his wife, little daughter and son, and told me that he was having the typical troubles at home that came from being away for long periods at a time.

His wife was getting ready to leave him because of it, and he knew it. If he didn't make it in tonight, he'd have to pick up his possessions from his front lawn; "One mechanical failure away from Divorce. " I said that I "knew that song" from my own family. It happens all the time in this business.

Using that particular phrase triggered a thought train in him and he was quiet for a good five minutes. It was the first time in an hour, or maybe a couple of years that he hadn't looked dead-dog tired.

After a bit, he told me that he'd played trumpet when he was in high school. Said that he'd been in a band that wasn't any good, but had sure been a hell of a lot of fun. He wondered where, exactly, his trumpet was.

The independent long haul trucker is as scarce as the travelling merchant, the real Cowboy, or the Deep-water fisherman. A redeeming job, a kind of Craft that is, for whatever the reason, no longer acceptable to the public. A career without a suit is unfashionable. Not in good taste, or something. Passion is unnerving. Those are scarce now too. The tyranny of the masses strikes again.

The loss of self and family is almost a universal truth for those whose "jobs" are their lives. "A Man is what he does" is thought of as retrograde thinking. With the application of a long practiced trade, and the need to support a family that can always use more money, they are driven to be away from home. Sacrifice for a solitary art-form that only the perceptive, the patient, or those who have been there can understand.

A job, done well to the point of craftsmanship, can be more important than your life. A man is his work. You do it because you have to, because you have to do your best. Ask a cop, or a Firefighter. That's all there is, I think.

The culture barely understands that anymore. It isn't considered polite. You clock out and that's all there is, hang up your uniform. Independence and persevering strength can hurt people, and they are in bad taste these days. The old-time-tough guys who miss half a day's work, over twenty years, for the funeral of a spouse just don't exist anymore. I don't know whether that's good or not.

Brad let me out a little before Ogalalla, Nebraska, because the radio said he had to pass through a D.O.T. inspection station a few miles ahead and the company had a strict "No Riders" policy.

I wished him well and he fished two bucks out of a paper cup of toll money on the dash to "buy a cup of coffee" (sacrament of the open road) at the next truck-stop.

I had about ten dollars to start with when I left Denver, and had spent a buck and some change on soda pop and crackers to christen the trip. The two bucks really helped.

I tried to refuse it from politeness and he told me that "only a fool turned down free money". There is courtesy, and there is survival. Give and take. Pass it along later. This was courtesy, and I tried to be gracious.

The truck-stop at the bottom of the exit ramp looked inviting, but I had been stuck there once before, five years earlier, listening, while I waited for a money order that never came, to the story of a waitress whose boyfriend had forty three more days left to go on the state road crew. They had been traveling too. Keep moving.

I watched the truck go out of sight, fading in the clear Nebraskan late afternoon, and thought that by the time I made Ogalalla he would be home, trying to make some peace. I wished I wore a hat, so I could tip it in his direction.

I started walking east.

Chapter 6

Road Song

"A man ain't an island, John Donne wasn't lying."
- Hard Day on the Planet, by Loudon Wainwright III

"He's got interstate running through his front yard,
and he thinks he's got it so good."
Pink Houses - John Mellencamp

Having grown up, as I said, in the microcosmic 'burbs of Massachusetts, where the main streets of some towns I lived in, really had, just like legends say, once been cow-paths, I suppose I should have been a little nervous or something about walking down a highway in Nebraska. It's BIG out there. No walls or trees close.

Agrophobia, agoraphobia, I think it's called something like that; the fear of open space. I always thought it sounded like a sick dread fear of farmers. The next town was out of sight over the horizon. The sky was about a hundred and eighty degrees high and three sixty around; a perfect bowl of sky.

I remembered the first time that I'd ever really experienced the sheer, actual, SIZE of Nebraska. I'd driven all night, through the comfortable little repeating sine wave valleys of Iowa, formed by the generous glaciers that made that fertile land, and woke up next to a truck-stop gas station that was the only thing above ground level besides me for as far as I could see. I remember looking at a field of what is, if you're from there, pretty normal sprouting corn, and thinking, "You could put most of Boston right there". I think my mind went a little strange.

When you live in the little Victorian drawing room and Puritan workspace towns of New England. The largest space you ever get to see is from a mountain up in New Hampshire or Vermont. If not that, the biggest open space you see is a park, a football field or maybe a Highway.

Sky limits itself in the trees, which, in the distance everywhere, are always black.

The difference is really only noticeable if you are not used to it. After you live in a huge preplanned western city, like Denver or L.A., you get acclimated to six lanes of traffic in each direction inside the valley's city sprawl, and thirty or forty mile views out on the plains. You don't get that kind of space 'Back East'. Even the ocean follows the curve of the earth. I've tried to explain how big The West is to people from back home. They have a hard time grasping the idea that there is land that nobody has ever owned and places where there isn't a tree for over a mile. You can only wait and hope that they will come see it themselves.

I don't even attempt to describe Moab.

There was a song back in the sixties or seventies about the phenomenon as it effected Colorado. It said, in part, "Bring your festivals and dope, bring your Winnebagos, and your money too, just don't forget to leave when you get through."

Walking felt good, and I wished I knew how to do handsprings down the breakdown lane for the freedom and openness of the place. I thought about dancing, and couldn't figure out how to keep it from looking like psychosis or a seizure.

About an hour later I came to a generic fast food rest area and had dinner. These things grow like weeds, like missionaries of messy civilization to the clean openness of the plains society of grass. Like crabgrass on a suburban lawn in 1964 New Rochelle.

I want to find the little corporate weasel who keeps spreading the seeds. It was probably the same guy who ordered the thousand acres of South American rain forest a day to be turned into pasture: fucked up the ecological balance so badly that it was turned into a desert. I want to have a long talk with that little corpo-speak geek. Maybe investigate whether they mean it when they put those "Inedible Grease" stickers on the waste boxes out back.

Thirty or fifty years ago there would have been a little Mom & Pop diner out here, a knocked together shack probably, or maybe a post-war Quonset hut or a stainless steel Pullman car; just barely sanitary by modern standards. The menu would have had meatloaf with mashed potato and gravy as Thursday's Blue Plate Special.

I know of one on the East Coast like that, but I'm keeping the location a secret because the owner is a frustrated former European pastry chef, and the blue plate special is just a front for the deserts. Ever had a meatloaf blue plate and a glass of milk followed by a

30

German Chocolate black cherry and truffle torte? The secrets of these places are revealed only to the initiate and the Lucky Traveller.

The Traveller often is cursed to spend the rest of his life looking for the place again. You can almost never predict what the specialty of the house will be. There are places in Lauderdale, Florida and Lyons, Colorado that make 'clam chowda' that'll rival anything in Boston or even Maine. I'm told that, before mass distribution of the top five carbonated beverages became almost mandatory for restaurants, the way to spot the really good diners was by the beverages. The choices would have been coffee, water, locally produced milk or, if the town was lucky, soda-pop.

A lot of small towns had their own local brand of carbonated beverage. The Birch Beer from Lucky Strike Bottling in Nashua, New Hampshire was one of my favorites. Tom Sawyer Root Beer in Massachusetts was pretty good too.

Soda or Pop they call it in the West. When I was a kid they called it Tonic. Hell, some of the brands that are still around started as "Tonics". "Moxie" was supposed to give you just that. 7-Up started out as "Lemonated Lithium". Active ingredient Lithium Carbonate. Target marketed at the overworked housewife. "Perky", indeed. Coca Cola's name speaks for itself- or did until about 1906.

The names are just names and don't mean anything but product recognition and marketing plans now, but history lends perspective. Think about everything, it will give you something to do when there's nothing on television.

I had a uniformly produced little meal in a polystyrene coffin, sitting cross-legged among the tall grasses on a manhole cover over the drainage ditch. The plastic box from the plastic restaurant was okay., but the plastic people were just too much. There aren't supposed to be any robots in Nebraska. I mean it ain't the citadel of advanced philosophy and bioengineering, but this was pushing the limits. There was moss and a few tenacious frogs in the culvert, so there was hope.

The sunset was one of those glorious blue and red tinged salmon pink and pale orange things that happen across about a hundred miles of sky all at the same time. Salmon pink like a fish, a living, wriggling fish, not like out of a can; fine and subtle gradations of amazing colors that I could never describe in full.

A western sunset is a terrible thing. I hate them. They are so beautiful that you can't ever really watch one and be the same again. It just wrecks your heart to see something so indescribably perfect, so fleeting and yet so huge. You can't ever go back. All the works of thousands of years of human toil couldn't make anything like a western sunset. You can't ever even make anything big enough to obscure it. Pollution even makes 'em better.

They have these every day.

Best thing about the place was that sunset and the sound of the crickets just tuning for the evening symphony. The rustling grass was nice. Stars and wind for accompaniment.

All my calories and food groups had been carefully counted, thought out and planned. I could have a meal that tasted just exactly like this here individual meal unit in New York, London, Tokyo, Beijing, Paris or, as of six months before, Moscow. Made it feel somewhat, uh, un-unique.

I thought about great and glorious meals that I have had. Meals that have spent half a day cooking on an old gas or wood stove, or in the coals of a campfire, and would not have been half so good without their compliment of wood-smoke, love and soot.

Stuff with too much fat and salt and cholesterol and starch. Red meat and heavy whole wheat bread. Soft butter the color of a daisy's heart. Vegetables that actually grew in rich black dirt and apple pie from the tree out back. Old family recipes and clever bits of innovation and last minute improvisation. Meals that have damned little regard for hygienic, portioned little smears of processed "mayonnaise-food" and "cheese food product" on little tiny pieces of spongy alleged bread with a sugar content above five percent.

Steinbeck got a bit peeved over jelly in "little plastic coffins" and the "sanitized for your protection" toilets. (I read somewhere that the place you are most likely to get a staph infection is a hospital.) He took umbrage at the idea of disposable plastic motel drinking glasses. He never imagined that food "Untouched by human hands!" could be a good thing. I guess I see his point. Crocodile Dundee said, "You can live on it, but it tastes like shit". That's about true.

Old John never imagined that it could get any worse. That mankind could ever be further removed from his humanity than it was when he took his trip. Sad to say, the progression of alienation continues unabated. Someday we may not touch the Earth at all. We

32

still have rich earth some places and, for the moment anyway, we still have the sunsets.

Hard as it might be to imagine, I mean no slight to the fast food places of that ilk. They perform a function, but they seem to have no soul.

They are better than no food at all, but if you are in a greasy little mom & pop diner somewhere far from wherever home is, and your heart is heavy, maybe you can hear a song on the jukebox, or the old grease coated Bakelite radio next to the grill that means something to you and might be able to get you through.

Duffel bag, backpack, or suitcase, it's all the same in the light of the dusty neon in the *greeeezy* cafes. Echo chamber Country or Blues down on the A.M. band.

We as Americans, more or less, or maybe just as universal denizens of the last portion of the 20th Century were raised, at least partly, in the backs of station wagons, between the Dairy Queen rest stops and the A & W Root Beer stands. Holding in back-pressure hotdog burps induced by Coca Cola and potholes are one of the few commonalties we have.

Even if we never did those things in real life with our families or friends, we saw them on television. We know that they're real feelings.

The radio is another one. If you meet somebody from somewhere else, almost anywhere else, you can rest assured that they heard some of the same music you did.

A friend of mine uses a thing called "Radiomancy" as a divination tool. "Bibliomancy" is the practice of opening a bible to a random place to seek advice from God. Depending on your orientation, some say it can it can work with other books. It's a synergistic divination process of sorts that can give you a laugh, a piece of advice or divine commentary on your actions. It works better in very human surroundings. In the world most of us live in, radios are more common than Bibles.

In a fast-food joint, you would be lucky to get a canned version of "the theme from M.A.S.H.": which is called, if you remember your history, "Suicide is Painless". I heard it once in a franchised "Italian food" restaurant (which, needless to say, bore little resemblance to the cooking of my Italian relatives or friends), and I asked the management about it.

They said canned music was very popular because it helped the clientele digest. He said he'd been there so long, himself, that he didn't even notice it anymore.

I suppose that about says it all on that topic.

Chapter 7

Meet John Doe

"And now for something completely different..."
- John Cleese, Monty Python

My Dad's buddy John came to stay with us for a while when I was a kid. He was a truck driver, and his name really was John Doe. When he'd had Cop trouble as a kid it had made him really popular. The name gave him a sort of a natural predilection for being a smartass.

He was a city boy, and he came by it naturally. It probably wouldn't be all that notable, if the city in question weren't Sommerville, Massachusetts. Sommerville is one of those blue-collar Yankee industrial towns that have a long sub-literate history.

Makes Lowell look glamorous. French toast is one of those fancy foreign dishes. It has folk legends and oral histories that contain truisms like "don't ever fuckin fight with goddamn mongoloids, those fuckers are tough bastards" and "don't read too many books or you'll get so smart you can't think".

It's still, according to him, a step above Medford and Everett. He was, perhaps, just a little too much the wise guy for his own good, but I always figured it was a desire to be a country boy, rather than an exile that had driven him from his homeland. I asked him, and he said he was truck driven out of there. Hard to keep 'em in Paree, when they've seen the farm...

At the time he'd had some troubles with the lady he'd been living with, and a bit of trouble with his wife as well. He described his wife's way of looking at the world as "having a friend meant you always got somebody to hit up for lunch money". This, he said, could make anybody move to New Hampshire.

It seems the girlfriend was having a thing with a police officer in the small town where she lived, and John was a little put out by it. In fact he came over one night and found out that his clothes, tools, beer can collection and all his George Jones records had been put right out in the snow. At the time he was a little buzzed out, so he just loaded all the stuff into his "genuine Husky & Starch" Torino, and went to see his wife.

Where the problem came in was that he got to thinking on it, which he swore was always a dangerous activity that never leads anywhere good.

His mind ran over and over an inventory of things he'd given her, and things of his that must still be in her house. The missing items kept coming back into his mind, and after he got in from the road that Friday, he stopped in at the bar and had a couple. And then a couple more.

The problem, he deduced, was not only his missing television, cast iron pans, and his favorite shotgun, but that goddamned little cop. So he got to thinkin' and drinkin' and a plan began to form in his mind. By about midnight he had it nailed down solid.

When John's Torino, (red, with a white swoosh- limited edition factory reproduction of the car from the TV show "Starsky & Hutch") with a bandana masking the license plate, did the smoking bootleg turn in middle of "Ye Olde Towne Centre", as the city fathers insisted on calling it, his opposite number, The Cop, couldn't resist. He hit the siren and the lights and probably cursed the aforementioned "Towne" fathers for giving him a stodgy, taxi cab looking, Checker Marathon as a Police Car, rather than a nice sporty Camaro.

When John started turning donuts around the war memorial, tires screaming and effectively clouding the square, the cop surely decided that the ban on Hot pursuit could be effectively disregarded if it became necessary. Purely as a matter of public safety.

When the flashing red and white Torino crossed the curbing into the Town Common, Officer Friendly had decided that, if he could just catch the son of a bitch, he'd ram him until the Torino looked like a beer can under a tractor tire.

When John's car began the series of graceful figure eights, Officer Friendly's reaction could only be testified to by whoever does his laundry.

The Mighty Red Torino had almost rammed him, but had only passed close enough to splatter his already humiliating new Checker Police Car with fresh mud and new mown grass.

When John began the carefully planned clockwise circuit around the newly installed playground area in the middle of the common, his victim's reaction was better than could be expected.

Instead of following him wide around and rolling the cruiser out and over on it's passenger side, Officer Friendly cut it too close before making the turn and rolled the cruiser right through the newly installed playground equipment.

Or at least partially through it, as he only made it approximately as far as the middle of the jungle gym set.

John's next step was, of course, to pick up the rest of his stuff. The former girlfriend in question seemed not to be in attendance when he arrived. And he figured that since he'd had to make so much noise kicking in the goddamned door because, for some reason, his key wouldn't fit, that he'd be sure to get her attention if she was. He said that failure to be able to work a door, was a sure sign that you need to watch your beer consumption.

He headed for the kitchen first, and gathered together his pans, and recovered a case of beer from the fridge that he had completely forgotten about somehow. It wasn't his regular brand, but, hey, beer is beer. On his way to the living room to get the shotgun he turned on the television for the last time, as a way of saying goodbye.

As he got the treasured shotgun, with it's walnut stock and inlaid silver, down from the pegs over the fireplace he heard, over a brand new police scanner on the kitchen counter, the sound of Officer Friendly, describing him, his registration numbers and possible intricacies of parentage, to the State Troopers and a couple of surrounding departments. John knew what he had to do.

He sat down on the couch and cracked a beer. He took the shells out of the coffee table drawer and, carefully loaded both barrels.

The television, was a big color set that he'd purchased so they could watch old movies, cartoons and football together. He'd been fond of it, back when he was fond of her. It chatted amiably at him about his rings around his collar. Kind of like her.

No way out. Nothing else to do. No other solution. BOOM!

Sent that sucker to live in heaven with Jesus and Elvis.

Then he made what he refers to as his biggest mistake. He fell asleep on the couch.

According to, a now repentant, and long-time-sober John, a number sixteen cast iron skillet makes a rather disappointingly shallow "thup" sound when it gongs off the side of your skull. But it is, he tells me, a remarkable fact that any object that is thrown, swung, lobbed or hurled by a scorned, angry, PMSing, or otherwise pissed-off woman, has a chance of hitting the mark that is directly proportional to the cumulative amount shit she has had to take from you. He says the odds are even better if she sneaks up on you.

He says that for a really good ringing sound, which is at least in some relation to the inherent amount of pain involved, you need to use stainless steel. I'm not sure how he went about gathering that last bit of information, but when he woke up from the impact of the pan, Officer Friendly and the former girlfriend were putting him into the back of the now right-side up police car.

We were living in Andover at the time, and my dad got him a job where he was working. John came to stay with us shortly after he finished the two hundred and seventy days that the judge gave him for, according to John, discharging a gun in the house, even though he was just cleaning it, suspicion of dangerous driving, and being an asshole within the city limits.

` I've seen the transcript of the trial. The word "fuck" cost him 60 days. Twice.

One morning in January, shortly thereafter, he and my dad were getting ready to go to work. I was getting ready for school. It was early, and the sun was just about up.

John folded the collar of his flowered shirt down over his denim jacket, ran the switchblade comb through one last time, and he was ready. The straight-legged jeans over his custom cowboy boots were washed to the same shade as the jacket. He's a wiry little guy who is a dead ringer for Jerry Reed and his sense of fashion was a lot like his diction: indigenous to his homeland. Besides, it was the seventies. He went out to warm up his prized Torino while Dad was in the shower.

It was less than a minute before he came back in looking excited, and pounding on the bathroom door for my dad.

"Hey Jack, dere's some little fucka out heya destroyin' yer truck."

My Father's two-tone blue Ford pickup (With fiberglass cap, fat wheels and tires, Mack bulldog and Thrush side-pipes) was his pride and joy. To fuck with it would be an unpardonable sin.

It was less than a minute before he came hurtling out of the bathroom, pants buttoned but not belted, boots on but not laced. At a bit over six feet and two fifty, moving like a nose tackle, it was a significant sight.

He's had a beard since a "youthful indiscretion" wrapped him and a black fifty-three Ford coupe around a small stand of maple trees, and it was still full of shampoo foam from the shower.

In that intervening minute, John had gone off, with notable joy, to warn the kid that his death was imminent. The kid was my age, and a paperboy, but I'd only seen him around, and didn't know him. That chrome Mack bulldog must have been just a little too tempting.

When I looked out to see what was going on, John had cornered the kid against a snow bank a few hundred yards up the street, where he sat on his bicycle after his ill-fated escape attempt.

The Torino was nose-in to the snow bank, so, other than up, there was only one way out, and that was past John. I could see the kid look at his escape route, and realize that the thing that looked like a bear charging out of the front of the building was coming for him.

The old man got into his truck, fired it up, and tore out in a plume of snow and exhaust roar, straight for John and the kid.

The kid looked nervous, from what I could see, I could sympathize. John was talking to him, and a kid from a nice little town like Andover had probably never been threatened in native Somerville-eese. It must have sounded, allowing for the splintered phrasing, like a conversation with the KGB or the Federales.

John was telling him, according to the version of the story I heard later, "Big Jack's gonna kill ya. He killed the last guy ta fuck wit' his truck, an' he'll kill you too. Tied 'im to the back and dragged 'im to Revere. Now he's gonna kill ya. He's gonna rip off your arms, beat ya ta death with 'em, tear off your head an shit down your throat. Then he's gonna desecrate yer fuckin copse."

My view of the kid was obscured by the pickup sliding into place to make up the third side of the triangle. I can only imagine the poor kid's horror at seeing foam dripping from the beard of this two hundred and fifty pound tattooed nightmare.

You do something wrong and get caught, you get yelled at. Worst case there might be reparations. Having your corpse desecrated sounded like it was going to be unreasonable.

The kid had been doing something bad and he knew it from the start. He had just been warned, fled fairly, and been captured anyway. Now this hairy monster, wearing no shirt in the middle of January was coming to kill him. Doom. Imminent, immediate painful doom.

John was enjoying the hell out of the whole thing. He'd enjoyed scaring the hell out of the kid more than probably anything else he'd do all week, and my father, seeing that the damage was pretty minimal must have gotten into the spirit of the thing. There are certain George & Lenny aspects to the relationship.

To get all the way out here and find that it was an eleven year old on a bicycle was disheartening. That the only damage was an easily fixable crease in the hood must have made it worse.
You can't hit him, you can't slam his fingers in a desk drawer, but yelling at him would not convey the point adequately.

My father hit upon what was, considering the circumstances, a fairly elegant solution. He picked the kid up and inserted him, newspaper pouch and all, up to his chin, into the snow bank that the plows had made during the night. It was sort of anticlimactic, but certain to be effective to some degree.

A thing like that has got to at least catch your attention. To make sure that it remained fresh in the little thief's mind, or perhaps just to do the job thoroughly, he inserted the bike, one handed, and wheels down, right next to the kid. Like a dead king going to the afterlife with his horse, the kid was buried, arms pinned to his sides, with his all worldly goods.

The next thing I saw was the old man, partially frozen shampoo still dripping from his beard like a rabid dog, come around the truck, dusting his hands off, and get back in. He drove back to the house and finished his shower.

Jeremiah Johnson had recently been the movie of the week on television, and John had some claim to a bit of Indian blood. I knew both of them had seen the movie. The scene where Redford comes across the trapper that the Indians have buried up to his chin must have caught their fancy.

John, last I saw of him before pulling my head in to keep from getting caught watching all of this, was up on the snow bank, walking around and around the kid's head, packing the snow. His hands were moving, so I knew he was talking. He was probably telling the kid how lucky he was that Big Jack hadn't fuckin' desiccated and then killed him.

On my way to school a bit later, I noticed the hole in the snow bank, and the footprints and the tracks of the bicycle leading away from the scene. They looked, if such a thing is possible, humble.

Chapter 8

Nebraska Night

"There are nights when the wolves are silent
and only the moon howls."
- George Carlin

Time to face the Muzak. The sun would be down in half an hour, and I kind of wondered what it would be like to sleep in the tall sweet grasses amid yellow and green chamomile at the side of the road.

Motion is addictive.

I got back out there on 80, the super-slab, and started walking toward a distant black roadside tree, branches stretched aloft like fine nerves, a few miles distant. Maybe that's what western roads are, trees in the distance that look like nerve endings under a microscope.

I really do hate these sunsets. This one had finally gone a really sublime pink and champagne color. These things wreck me, and sometimes they are all there is to keep me from giving in to the compulsion for plastic. It was just about too dark to keep going when a little brown Renault stopped for me.

His name was Wiley and he made a point of spelling it for me. A limber little old guy, he seemed happy and pretty well adjusted to life.

The car was loaded down with heavy cable working gear and he drove loosely at seventy-five to eighty with his bare left foot on the dashboard. A broad gestured driving style only possible when you get used to living in big space. We drove all night and he told me that he built ski lifts for a living. He said that he had just fallen into it a long time ago and did pretty well.

He was originally from, approximately, East Germany, though he was old enough to have been born before that was a relevant distinction. His soft German accent was laced with something like lowland Scots or Liverpool English. It did not seem polite to ask the reasons for such a combination. If I thought about it long enough I could guess.

We discussed the LA Riots, and the general state of the world for most of the night. We talked about school, education, and how lax and impolite most Americans are for not thinking the learning of other languages is important.

I felt a little backward and provincial myself, possessing only colloquial American English, enough Spanish to get myself killed, a little ex-Catholic Latin and the smattering of other stuff that you just pick up. He said that's just the way it is. I'm still a bit embarrassed about it.

We concluded that the way to solve the problems of the world was to find a way to give people back their sense of responsibility for their actions.

No cop-outs: you do the crime, you do the time. The idea that there is punishment for crime is supposed to be one of the deterrents to crime.

I'm not talking Draconian Les Miserables stuff here, but responsibility for personal action. No fake-out Insanity Plea that will have you back on the street a week after you commit a crime. Publish the names of the parents of kids who get caught carrying guns to school.

Make it clear to kids that if you work hard in school, and don't get into trouble, that there is something more than unemployment and bullshit to look forward to. Then make the system work like that.

Jail is the place you go if you commit a crime. The nature of crime is an interesting topic, though.

There are victimless crimes (possession of drugs for your own use, prostitution, free speech), which should be a slap on the wrist. Then there are heinous crimes (intentionally killing an innocent person, intentionally harming a child, intentionally fucking up an ecosystem) for which you should be taken out and shot like a rabid dog.

I guess it's all a matter of where you come down on the purpose of incarceration: is it rehabilitative or punitive? The system is a bit confused in many places.

The "War on Drugs", for example, is bullshit: as is the property seizure that goes with it- but that's what democracy is for: if a law is bad, change it.

It seemed normal enough to him that I was hitching cross-country to go to school. European thing, I guess.

Sometimes we were quiet, and thought about what we'd said, or just thought, which is a rare enough thing these days. It was an agreeable and rare way to have a conversation.

There is a kind of penetrating starlit blackness to the Nebraska night that must be a lot like the deep stillness of outer space. Nothing between you and the distant suns of other galaxies but space and time. This is said to be flexible, and in the vast Midwestern night you can believe it.

An isolation that makes everything feel close and far away at the same time. Go anywhere, all the time, and it bears a resemblance not only to where you've been, but where you are going. A continuum with the ability to make Einstein chuckle in his frayed sleeve.

Neon pink cars, stegosaurus Cadillacs, The Great American Road. Stephen Hawking would love it as a concept, and Newton would worry about discontinuity in its linear surface (potholes). Richard Feynman had a van painted in Feynman Diagram hieroglyphics: he really knew how to go with the flow.

What's out here? A lot of stuff, but really nothing. Billions and billions of something, but what?

You can watch the clouds skate the surface of the planet like breath on a mirror. You can almost touch the stars. They tick by like points in a Stargate: Shelton, Lincoln, York, McCool Junction, Papillion. The rhythm of the road becomes inaudible beneath the roar of the solar wind; there is only flow and weightless drift. Orbiting Grand Island and sling-shotting from its gravity well. Now approaching the planet Omaha. Prepare for a extreme temporal distortion.

As we drove through what Bruce Springsteen knowingly called "That Dark Nebraska Night", which is really a sort of state of the soul that can be anywhere, I thought about why people go other places and realized I had no answers to anything.

Nothing at all. Like the Zen masters, walking their roads barefoot, you bargain with yourself for the last of your own baggage and, eventually, realize how little you really need. Stuff just slips away out here. You don't miss it: you don't need it.

Wiley and I talked about political goofballs and humanity, about decadence and living well (as a process), cars and boats (he was restoring a 1928 Chris-Craft cigarette boat with oak and mahogany and a Packard engine. I wished I could see that.) We had a discussion of the design aspects of Deloreans versus Cords, and a few anecdotes about Post War three wheeled automobiles. Trihawk wins over the BMW Isetta every single time.

At dawn he dropped me off at Corralville, Iowa, just outside of Iowa City. A town that looks, more or less like all the rest of the Midwest in the daylight.

He turned off to head up to the rich dells of Wisconsin. Before he was even out of sight I thought of a dozen more things to discuss with him.

Chapter 9

Henry

"Every man has his secret sorrows which the world knows not;
and often times we call a man cold when he is only sad."
— Henry Wadsworth Longfellow

It was six thirty in the dew soaked Eastern Iowa morning, and I had made pretty good time for somebody whose major mode of transport had laces. I walked inland to the nearly legendary "Buckeye Rapid Relay Station" and had eggs, pancakes, toast, juice and coffee for about three dollars. Almost couldn't finish it all. I've talked to a dozen different people who have been passing through Iowa over the last 20 years and have happened to wander in there. They don't know why either.

I read the house papers (New York Times, USA Today, Des Moines Register) and looked at the display racks of glossy post cards: ears of corn larger than tractors, outhouse jokes, and pictures of cows driving cars. They had refrigerator magnets of all the states. No Jackalopes, though.

There was a fellow named John Patric who traveled around back in the thirties. Another brother of the open road, he wrote a book called "Yankee Hobo In The Orient", which is now long out of print.

A journeyman printer, Patric did odd jobs and saved his money. Got together a hundred and eighty bucks back in '37, and went to Japan and China to see what it was really all about.

In those days in Asia you could travel and live like a king for about a dollar a day. Stories of Singapore have a decadence that seemed to scare the Westerners who were there.

None of that for this guy, though: Patric went native and lived on about two cents a day. Had several interesting adventures and formed his own opinions. He was probably the only Westerner to see the "Grand and Mystical Orient"™ at street level, where the real people are, before it all changed. Back when it was as foreign and distant a land as there was. He wrote down the story of his trip, and you can learn enough about the man from his honest way of looking at things as you can from the fact that he typeset and printed all the copies of the first seven editions himself.

A stubborn and honest man, that Patric, I always wondered what happened to him. His standing offer, in one of the book's many digressions, was to lease, only to like-minded people, some land for a buck a year, or a pail of blackberries. He also had a pretty good recipe for cooking fish on the exhaust manifold of a moving car. His book once saved a life that I'm fond of, and I really want to thank him. Maybe send him some blackberries.

I was, after a good deal of the usual procrastination, back out on the road by eight thirty. I walked about a mile and was just getting into my long-walking pace when I got to the next exit. It was the one for the University of Iowa and I was trying to remember what the hell the significance of the place was, and whether or not it would be worth taking a break to go in to have a look around.

At the beginning of the exit ramp, I was looking at a 1972 motorcycle license plate, a woman's little short sock with a pink fuzz-ball at the heel, and a fan belt, seemingly unbroken. All next to an oil stain on the cracked breakdown lane pavement. Closer, the tiny diamonds of safety glass, four cigarette filters, a birch beer bottle cap and a weathered scrap of red bandanna lay piled on the bottom half of the cover of a slick romance novel.

I tried to piece together the story that they had to tell and remembered that the U. of Iowa was where the Writer's Program was. Damn. The little bell rings: Hard return.

Of course! Some kind of Taoist billboard. Some wonderful stuff had been written around here.

There was beige foamy looking pollution on the small river that I crossed between the two exits and wondered how anyone could be inspired by a river that was so obviously and grossly polluted. What the hell would Wallace Stegner say?

I was thinking about a foreign exchange student who I'd read about during finals a while back. He had flipped out and shot a couple of people here. I wondered if it was the pressure of finals or the sight of that river that caused his madness. Some places in the world can't squander the resources we do.

At Columbia University, in 1969, a student ran through the library with a gun trying to get students to stop studying because they were getting ahead of him. Final exams are rough.

An old Ford pickup pulled over to pick me up and I got in gratefully, after all, it was finals week in back in Denver.

An aluminum camper shell on the back and a blue plastic bug guard on the front. Generic brown semi-metallic off the rack paint job with one upgrade every ten years or so. Pragmatic. Iowa, man, people put a high value on sensibility here. None of the information overload you get in the megalopolic cities. No gibberishly rattling hundred and seventy cable channels here. The truck had Iowa license plates from one of the rural counties on it.

The guy driving the truck was older, a thin fellow in a blue down vest and a baseball cap from a farm machinery dealer from up in Des Moines. He was the kind of Okie angular thinness that another Romantic would call the look of the eternal Midwestern farm-belt: part hard moldboard plow tilling the earth with his gnarly cracked hands as his wind-worn face endures the sun and wind and rain from the relentless sky, the rest just plain stubborn. I wouldn't: I'd say he was more that kind of thin that is somewhere between the skeleton with muscles look that is called "rawboned" by the writers of Western Fiction, and the gaunt look of a prison camp survivor. To me he looked deeply tired.

He had a pillow covered in a white and yellow checkered percale, and an old paper and leather suitcase next to him on the seat. The suitcase was tied with a piece of clothesline. It sat like an old dog on a makeshift leash.

He said that his name was Henry and he went through the usual dance of asking me my name and where I was going, with the manner of people all over the world who pick up hitchhikers; politely veiled fascination and disinterest in the long version of the tale, or boredom: Either way it looks about the same. Two travelers on an unloved train, but the asking gave you something to do. He didn't seem like a guy who talked a lot.

When I asked him about his trip I had no idea that he was carrying as much baggage as he was. Henry said that he had been a Printer for the last thirty years and just couldn't do it anymore. Mental burnout and some health problems from, what he said. His wife was in a convalescent home in Davenport and she was dying. He said that he could not be there anymore and had to go somewhere.

This guy had seen a little too much lately and felt like he was going off to find a place to die. Perhaps he thought I'd kill him. You know what they say about hitchhikers.

He said that he knew he was pretty messed up and was kind of afraid of things. The front bumper of his truck had some clotted mud and grass on it from where he had driven off the road sometime during the night and he told me that he'd been trying to get out of the ditch for most of the morning.

We drove the rest of the morning and stopped at a couple of rest areas so that he could get out and walk around a bit. I stretched and thought about how to help this guy out. Some people in the cities tell a story about a girl named Kitty Genovese; I felt obligated.

He obviously did not really want to be going anywhere, but felt the need to go somewhere, to do something. It was almost as if he was attached to a large elastic band and the further he got, the harder forward motion became. Somehow, by default, he was going East. He'd made the courtesy of giving me a lift a high priority in his life.

At one point we stopped and he tried to buy me lunch at a franchised roast beef joint. It was nice of him, but not necessary. I sat with him and we talked while he ate. When I call up the memory, it feels like we were in a watercolor painting- some mixed media thing: either we were real, the place was translucent, and ethereal or the other way around.

A little later we stopped again and he saw a Chinese restaurant. He said that he had never had Chinese food and was really in the mood for a bowl of soup.

What he had in mind, I think, was his Mom's beef stew; something like that. Who knew how long she'd been gone?

He invited me to come in and have some food too. I declined and stayed in the truck to get some rest. I should probably have gone in and maybe helped him through the menu or something, but I just could not do it. Besides, how difficult could a Chinese restaurant menu in Iowa be?

At one point I got out of the truck and looked at a field that had been recently tilled. Spring, and this land was getting greener. There was thick humidity in the air, so strange after Colorado's dryness.

We were coming up on the Mississippi River and Henry's stops had been getting more and more frequent. It was like he didn't want to go any further but had made getting me to where I was going important. Good manners show in the little things.

He asked me a lot of questions about Vermont and New Hampshire and my family and what kind of trees and crops grew there. I told him, as best I could, about the things he asked. We talked a lot about fishing, though I don't know much about it.

I thought about things that I loved in that part of the world and told him. Things like maple sugaring time, and what the trees look like in the fall from the catwalk under French King Bridge in western Massachusetts. How the river looks like silver in the late afternoon sun. The way my grandmother's kitchen smells at Thanksgiving when three ovens are pressed into service for pies and turkeys and fresh bread. The time when the whole family comes home: gastronomically as richly textured as a Dylan Thomas story, and socially equivalent to an Irish Republican Army keg party without any guns or Protestants.

I hadn't been back home in over five years, but I was busy hoping that he would tell me about the things that he loved in his home.

He got to thinking about the things that he loved, and I could see by his eyes that most of them had turned on him and were hurting now. I guess love can be like that sometimes.

As we got closer and closer to the Illinois line and the grand and mighty Mississippi River, his driving got worse. You could almost reach out and twang that imaginary rubber band. There was road construction going on and we were restricted to one lane and fifty miles an hour. He drove at thirty-five.

At one point a bee flew into his open window and kept flying around in front of him. He batted at it with both hands and started yelling at it. I won't say what it was that he was yelling. Not because I have an over developed sense of storytelling; I won't tell because it was none of my business what he was yelling at whom. It was private.

After Henry and the bee got settled, he resumed driving at his normal pace and calmed down a bit. The bee settled on the edge of the driver's side window and I mentioned it to him so that he could just shoo it out. What he did was start yelling at it directly. He turned bodily in his seat, stamping down with both feet and started waving both hands at it like a jumping jack.

We must have been doing about sixty five or seventy and accelerating when we hit the angle iron sawhorse with the yellow flashing highway light on it. Then he stopped.

I can tell you what every scuff on that highway light looked like in intimate detail because it was coming right at me. Thank the Gods they don't use Jersey barriers out here.

The damage to the truck was minimal: The bug guard was shattered for about two feet, and the hood and grille, between the headlight and the radiator, had been pushed in about six or seven inches. The hood could still be opened and the radiator and headlight were unbroken.

He pulled in to the inside of the markers just barely in time to keep from being overrun by the trucks and cars coming up behind us. I'd gone as white as a sheet and wasn't really able to do much more than go around the truck when he asked me to drive for him. We could both feel his oppression as we got closer to LeClaire, the last Iowa town before the Mississippi.

When we got across that mile long bridge you could feel his imaginary rubber band part like old string or something. All the tension went out of him and he asked me to drive down into the town and look around.

He'd been to one of those wars in Asia once, but otherwise he had never been East of the Mississippi. We cruised through whatever the town is on the Illinois side while he, after asking me to tell him about Mark Twain and Tom Sawyer and Huck Finn, and all that. He told me about all the places that he's been fishing and the ways you cook different kinds of river fish and how good they tasted. He could be surprisingly eloquent about the subtleties of flavor and technique.

A couple of years earlier I'd stopped in a little burg somewhere near here on the river to do the old check oil, gas, tires, piss and grab a cup of coffee routine. Woman running the quickie mart told me how the local deputy sheriff had fixed a few things a while earlier so that she couldn't leave town. An unrelated death in the family, a foreclosure or two. No charges or anything like that, but a web of suspicion and responsibility that he maybe had something to do with.

She was in the midst of telling me more when the deputy came around to fill his thermos and make his morning advance on her. He looked like he was shooting fish in a barrel and not quite getting why he kept missing. He ran my out of state plate while he waited for me to go.

I didn't leave for over an hour. He sat in his cruiser. She stood behind the counter, too many years after the prom to believe she could really ever leave. I stood and listened and lit her menthol cigarettes. Nobody else came into the store.

She smoked. I smoked and drank coffee. The deputy, in his cruiser, smoked and drank coffee, glaring, trying to look bored. She talked. I listened. When I left I had a broken taillight that I never did replace.

I saw that quickie mart float away on television in the flood of '93. Fish in a barrel.

I finally left Henry in a rest area about thirty-five miles West of Chicago. He said he wanted to get some sleep and asked me to stay and he would drive me as far as he could get on the money he had. He showed it to me and it looked like about thirty dollars.

I gave him a small Lapis Lazuli that I had in my pocket for good luck. I figured he needed it more than I did. He said that he had never seen a rock so blue and pretty before

I'm not sure why I left him there, other than to say that it was what I did. I'm still not happy about it. There was something I was supposed to do or say that would make it all right or at least all right for him. I didn't know what it was. Still don't.

I think that he needed to go home and try to work things out. I listened and I knew that I couldn't be responsible for him. I did what I could and did not have the ability to take him any further. It wouldn't be fair to use him up. He'd make me responsible for his death somehow if I let him. Bleak man, very bleak.

I walked off down I-80 for a while trying to get him out of my mind. Finally, I sat down under an apple tree that grew on the side of the road to change my socks and have a drink from my canteen. East of the Mississippi, where the land does change somehow, the distant trees in are brown or tan, but hardly ever black. Maybe this is better than the plains of the West, somehow.

I kept thinking about a lady I once loved, a long time ago, who thought that she was dying. Eventually, she did.

I remember walking with her on a full moon night in a Colorado mountain town as we talked about work and other unimportant things. I remember her taking off her shoes to walk in

52

the grass under that enormous harvest moon and sticking her pretty face into late summer petunias in a small flower bed in somebody else's yard. I guess I used to embarrass more easily than I do now.

She told me to tell anybody who asked, after she was gone, that I had seen her kissing tiny flowers. Said that was how she wanted to be remembered.

I thought about what it must be like to die slowly, from the inside, and believe there was no stopping it. A dread fearful weight that doesn't ever let you go. Maybe like being caught in the eye of a cobra. You don't move because you know that you cannot possibly move fast enough, and besides, it's so fascinating.

Like a lot of other people in the days of A.I.D.S., and alcohol related traffic deaths over fifty thousand a year, I've lost a lot of friends. One hell of a lot of acquaintances, and a lot of friends.

People die. It's just the balance to the equation. But it hurts when it's one of your own: especially the good people, or one of the children. They can't help it.

Death is an equal opportunity event. One to a customer. Dying doesn't scare me much, it seems like a release: looking forward to dying scares me. Wanting to die scares me, because I often do. There are more important things to do first. Pain scares me. Dying slowly and not being in control of it scares the hell out of me. I have an organ donor card in my wallet that says: "Take what you need. Good luck." I hope it will work.

They say the old Eskimos would know when it was time, give away all their stuff, and walk away naked across the ice.

Allen Ginsberg said he'd seen the best minds of his time turn to mush, or something like that. I don't know if I know any of the best minds of my time, but that doesn't make them any less important.

I've lost friends to drunks on the wrong side of the highway, and to melancholia and meningitis, A.I.D.S. and amphetamines, cocaine and lust, Quaaludes and quack Doctors. In late '92 I lost one of my oldest friends to breast cancer. Fucking breast cancer is so treatable that they do it outpatient in an hour, but this lady had no insurance, so she died.

I'd be okay leaving Henry there, even if he died I guess, if it were not for the fact that when I was coming back, a month later. I looked over at the rest area where I left him. I thought I saw the back top corner of what looked like his truck. I did not stop.

I told this story, in it's entirety, to my friend Maryanne just a few minutes ago so that I could find a nice, convenient way to justify the whole thing. To wrap it up neatly for you, Dear Reader, if not for myself.

I guess I hoped that if I HAD gone back to see if he was still there that there would be no sign of him, and I could get myself to believe that he had just gone back home. What I was afraid of was that maybe that I'd find him sitting in his truck and crying, remembering, thinking, living on vending machine food like some sort of post-modern gypsy. I didn't stop.

Maryanne said, maybe because she does not have the barriers against possible realities that I guess I have, "you couldn't have, He might have had a gun in his glove-box". I don't know if she meant that he'd kill himself, or me, or what. I guess I should ask. Sometimes I have no idea what she means.

Whether or not I could have, the point is that I didn't, and I'm not sure I feel so good about that.

In Asia and India and most of America we ignore people in desperate need, for one reason or another. It's sort of a social convention to let the other guy work out his own Karma. This might be cruel or it might be just. It might just be Darwin. It may be used to justify any belief system you can think of, even the ones that think of themselves as kind. It may be better than pity, I don't know.

A guy once said that a good deed, an honorable action, was one that you don't feel bad about afterwards. In some way, I know I didn't do the right thing. Hell, I'm not even sure I know what the right thing would be.

Chapter 10

Springfield and Grok

"So, If yesterday had a future, this is, like, IT?"
- Graffiti, Muddy's Java Cafe, Denver 1992

"Welcome to the jungle, Baby"
-Guns n' Roses

I ate some granola and changed my shirt. I started walking again after the break under the forgiving apple tree and its drainage culvert. I put my cigarette butts in an empty beer bottle I found there, and got a ride almost immediately from a guy in a Japanese pickup with a red canoe on top.

We got stuck in traffic and talked for quite a while. I wish I could remember what about. The only thing I remember is that he was a cop who had been canoeing with his family. He had a sunburn.

He dropped me off at Harlem Avenue on the outskirts of Chicago.

Tangential thoughts of the sacred Chicago Blues, up from The Mississippi Delta, and out from Harlem, in New York: Birdland and Langston Hughes. The American Blues Brothers Club (once owned by Dan Akroyd and John Belushi) had a motto: "Drink Booze-Talk Loud-Hear Blues".

They filmed in Chicago, of all things, a movie called "Adventures in Babysitting". B.B. King got a cameo and the line: "Nobody gets out of here without singing the Blues". Sweet Home Chicago.

It was hazy hot, and I could feel a little bit of the lake in the air. I needed to walk for a while, more out of a need to think about things than simple masochism. Walking is how I think, and the rare opportunity to be accomplishing something while doing it could not be passed up. Work out all the big problems while hitching cross-country. Sure, it beats pacing, but what the fuck am I doing in the Midwest?

A couple of miles later, near a large sports arena or something with a big billboard advertising upcoming rock concerts, I passed a guy who was hitchhiking from Portland, Oregon to Springfield, Massachusetts.

He'd been at it for over a week and he had a terrible sunburn. Flakes of skin shedding like a leper. He said his mother was dying in Massachusetts and had to get back home. I lit his cigarette for him, gave him two of mine, and kept walking.

I got as far as Pulaski Avenue, idly thinking about the original doctor on the new Star Trek. Star Trek: The Next Generation. Cultural transitions of the paradigm: If all the bad stuff happens to Picard, is it a karmic atonement for Kirk's womanizing and cultural interference on the original show? That would allegedly be the classical Faludi/Feminist view, and that of several major religions.

The Dahli Lama is said to be a fan of the new Star Trek: which is, in and of itself a little hard to imagine. Maybe the Pope would lighten up a bit if he watched it too?

My thoughts and I sat down on a Jersey barrier that meant the lane was going to close like a sclerotic artery. Friggin' road repair is everywhere. I heard once that the Golden Gate Bridge is constantly being re-painted: if it were me, I'd paint it some other color at least once.

Springfield pulled up in a little car full of big music. The guy who was driving was listening to Guns 'n Roses at clean wall of sound top volume and had the word "Grok" carved into the dashboard of his car with a pocket knife.

Grok said that this was the last exit before the city got too heavy to pick up hitchhikers, and I felt lucky. Springfield moved from the front into the back seat with the guy's kids and I got in. The stereo played "Welcome to the Jungle", and Grok's three young children were delighted to have Springfield as new terrain on which to walk their plastic dinosaurs. Springfield sat there looking like an old and tolerant family pet; a yellow triceratops in his hair.

I asked Grok, over the music, if he was a Sci-fi fan. ("Grok" comes from the Robert Heinlein Novel " Stranger in a Strange Land" and, roughly, means: Get into or Internalize something in a sort of Martian/western Zen point of view.)

He said that he wasn't into much Sci-fi, other than that book, which he'd read more than ten times. He said he hoped that there

56

were really people like that somewhere, and I asked him if he'd ever heard of The Church of All Worlds, out in California. A group founded on the behavior of the characters in the book. He smiled and asked me more.

Trying not to evangelize: which is tough when telling somebody about a Church. Only fair when it's one that I haven't got an affiliation with. I'd run into a couple of them a while back, and I saw one of their unicorns at the circus once. Both seemed pretty cool.

He said that he hadn't heard of 'em, but was really interested in finding out more. Wanted to know "if they Groked things." I told him what I knew from what I'd read and heard, and told him where he was likely to find the magazine they publish. He looked intensely happy and tried to make the music louder but the knob was maxed.

He dropped Springfield and I off at the far side of Gary, Indiana. And, without turning down the music, thanked me profusely.

The folks at The Church of All Worlds are an interesting bunch. Most notably, they raise the unicorns, which look very similar to goats with one horn. Ringling Brothers, Barnum and Bailey Circus made a big deal out of them. They've been making a go of balancing the whole agrarian-hippie trip with Macintosh computers and various forms of high tech. Owls periodically hunt down their computer mice. Earth worshiping woodsy Pagans, yes. Luddites no.

I decided to take a break and sit beside the road for a while. Springfield got a ride almost immediately.

I sat for a while thinking about what had happened so far and wondered why all this stuff was coming at me so fast. Speed-metal. Thirty hours and a thousand miles with no sleep.

There was a mangled battery box cover from a tractor trailer leaning against the base of a highway sign: fuel permits from most of the eastern seaboard and a column of addition, in black enamel on the crushed road-scraped chrome: Highway taxes for each state; the total was a hell of a lot more than I made last year.

Graffiti from a stall at Charlie's Deli in Kenmore Square, Boston:

"Stop the world, I want to get off!"

Beneath that it says: "Hey, that sounds like a personal problem to me-Call Dr. Ruth, not NASA." Beneath that: "and fucking selfish too!"

The principal of diving is nearly entirely opposite that of the Chautauqua, a contemplative, sentimental journey of more restful times. Diametrically opposite is not quite right, because there are moments of intensely lucid focus. But you miss a lot.

The Dive is about velocity rather than discovery, or maybe discovery through velocity, and may be fundamentally flawed because of it. You find things in full impact gestalt. Or they find you. You might find the whole world in a grain of sand in your shoe or looking at a building shaped like any other building. That's your problem. Accelerate. Stop. Focus. The Universe or God or your karma or whatever will let you know if it wants your attention for something. If it has to grab you hard to get your attention, it might hurt.

I was into the kind of rhythm that the road can produce in your mind. It's a kind of loopy Zen state where the only constant is motion. You can deal with almost anything as long as it's moving, like in-flight refueling. I don't know if it's redeeming or not, but in slightly over twenty-four hours I had made nearly a thousand miles. Not too bad at all.

To think that I have friends who doubt their future employability because they don't have tattoos or body piercings. Everybody they know is trying to look like a cross between Barker's Hellraiser and Bradbury's Illustrated Man, and they wonder what's wrong with themselves for not spending their spare moments trying to figure out what part of their body to put a piece of metal through. Some people are in need of creative hobbies. Sometimes subtlety is just completely beside the point.

Kinetic souvenir of Neal Cassady and Brother Kerouac: Speeeeed. They were burnin' up the two-lane on jazz and Benzedrine in a forty nine Hudson. Kick down automatic and all. The mad flair of "Old-God" George Shearing and Billie Holiday. Charlie Parker, the evil little tubes of bennies, and fer-gosh-sakes, saxophones.

Today we have two hundred and ten mile an hour teched and chipped race cars ready to go on the show room floor. Speed metal, eight lanes and crystal meth. Five or six speeds plus overdrive. Keys of cocaine. Turbo charged, intercooled, fuel injected computer controlled warp drives. Mega-methamphetamines. Two hundred mile an hour superbikes straight from the factory in Japan.

Leave your Victorian Vincent and wild red Indian motorcycles in the history books and the museums of the old machines. Designer drugs that will pop your brain out the front of your forehead like a 400 grain .50 caliber hollow-point are the thing of the moment.

Jazz, how, uh, restful. Apple pie and ice cream? Twenty-two second polystyrene wrapped grunge-burger and a shake? No fries with that, count your change. Next!

Welcome to the tag end of the twentieth century.

"It tastes like shit, but you can live on it."

Chapter 11

Rhapsody

"Make me an angel that flies from Montgomery
Make me a poster of an old rodeo.
Just give me one thing that I can hold onto
To believe in this living is just a hard way to go."
Angel From Montgomery, performed by Bonnie Raitt,
written by John Prine,

My friend Rhapsody is, in her own words, "just a little punker chick from the Midwest". I met her in Denver when she bummed a match from me on the patio of a health food cafe. Got a Bachelor's in Abnormal Psych., and currently working on her MA: I suspect she'll use her friends as a thesis. Everybody needs a hobby.

She wears Doc Marten combat boots, a leather jacket with a "smiley face" that has been shot in the forehead, and blue & white cotton underwear from Sears. She smokes too much and has a cat named Grymalkin. Someday she'll probably be a vice president of a bank. I'm Probably the only person who has ever seen her Mensa membership card.

When I first knew her, she told me a number of times that she sees sex and the psyche as the way people really view themselves; a true mirror on the soul, inextricably linked, a Root password to the real identity. I finally rose to the bait one day and asked her what she meant, and, in the shiny-clean well-lit college corridor she told me.

She used to work in a dingy little phone room in a dingy town somewhere. They did the psychic chat and telephone sex bit. 976 numbers.

Let me clue you, nobody is anymore psychic because they are getting paid for it. Believe me, the girls don't look like they do on late night television. Nobody dresses like those ads for real, but hey, if you're willing to spend five bucks a minute, for psychics or sex, that's your own business.

I have to wonder if any legit Economists have done research on Social Darwinian trends using this stuff as proofs?

Rhaps was just out of high school, and had always had the innate virtue of suburban security to lend perspective. And she thought she was tough. She didn't mind having to walk to work when she couldn't afford the bus. It was an adventure then.

She had her first apartment away from the folks, and a phone, and a group of her own friends. Lost her virginity that summer, too.

The job at the clothing store didn't pay very well, and it bored her anyway. When the boss got caught stealing, she got canned as a matter of course.

She got the job on the phone line out of desperation to pay the rent. The old woman in the stretch pants, with the big diamond ring and the missing teeth, had told her, as cigarette ash fell unheeded, that all she had to do was talk dirty, Honey.

Rhapsody has a great imagination, always read a lot and I'd believe she was able to fake her way through the interview. It was a Thursday, a week and a day before the first payday, and she'd just be able to cover the rent.

Company policy said that if you hang up on a client who wants to stay on the line, you're fired. Period.

On her fifth day at the new job, she spent four hours acting the part of a nine-year-old girl seducing her Daddy. She did the voice for me and I had to make her stop.

The Bosslady said, with a cigarette dangling from a glossed pancake lip, that she did good, and would get referrals for that sort of work more often.

It rained that night, and Rhapsody walked for hours. Tears don't show in the rain. She said she looked at things in a new way after that. Things and people, and wondered about what must really go on behind their eyes. Ordinary things and ordinary people.

She says she'd never, ever, if she lived a hundred years, want to be psychic.

A few weeks later she moved back home for a while.

Chapter 12

"Dis is a Good Ride."

"And if they take your sleep away sometimes they give it back again.
Soft sleeves of sound attend the darkling harbor..."
The Bridge (The Harbor Dawn) by Hart Crane

The problem was, I guess, that I got a little overconfident. Shit, as they say, happens. Speed, natural or otherwise, will do that to you, every time. I should have taken a nap, right there on the side of the highway, in the shade of the freeway and the tall cool trees, and I was even willing to think about sleeping in the breakdown lane, trucks whistling past and all.

But there were a few hours of sunlight left and I figured that I had best make the most of them. Make hay while the sun shines, and all that shit about high productivity they stick in your head when you're a kid. The Puritan Work Ethic is supposed to be good for you.

I got about five miles before I came to the beginning of a one-lane road construction project that was going to be fourteen miles long. Oh, great. Nice time to be an achiever. I guess you have to rebuild the infrastructure, but do they have to do it in the here and now?

I got out my sign that said "East", and figured that I'd either spend the night on the side of this road or be hitching again, for real, in about two and a half, three hours. Hup, Two, Three, Four.

A ratty little black Lynx wagon just sort of materialized in front of me. I really hadn't expected anyone to stop once I got inside of the orange cones leading up to the barriers, so I was just walking on a wide, blocked-off lane. Almost walked right into it.

I've never turned down a ride while hitchhiking. I guess it's either that I'm overconfident about my size (six feet and a good bit over two hundred pounds), the basic goodness of humanity, or that I'm just too lazy to walk. Either that, or I am a damned fool with absolutely terrible judgment and fabulous luck.

I guess I should have realized that my internal radar was not reliable at that point. Drunk drivers say things like that, afterward, too.

He was a pudgy guy, about five-seven and four feet around, wearing polyester pants and a sort of poly-cotton, madras-print, short sleeved shirt from a Wal-Mart sale rack.

The very first thing he said was that I'd have to ride in the back seat and put my stuff in the very back of the car. He was intent on this system of order to a point that would make a reasonably rested person fairly... okay, exceedingly, nervous. But fourteen miles of highway, at sunset, near a big, potentially dangerous city like Chicago didn't sound like a whole lot of fun.

I never did get his name right. He was a little guy in polyester driving a little econo-box with a muffler that was less substantial than my grandmother's lace curtains. How dangerous could he be?

I didn't hear his name very well, because he was talking through his nose. He said that he could not talk much because he had just come from surgery at the V.A. in Chicago, where they had done a nose job on him and he had these stitches in between his lip and nose, see? It looked kind of like he had ants.

I'm sorry, Dear Reader, If I sound a bit judgmental in my description. I know the whole rap about making snap judgments and all that, and I'm not, I think, what I'd call overly prejudicial. I am a bit wired from all this coffee, but that has nothing to do with it. You see, I'm also not always what you might call very bright.

I can, in retrospect, see the stupid slack grin on my face, when I've done something I should have thought through more. Sometimes the look sours in the middle of doing something stupid, the way it must if you find yourself parachuting down the side of a building after adjusting the patio umbrella on a rooftop table. The way Lou Costello, Buster Keaton and Harold Lloyd must have felt on a regular basis. You get so that you can feel the kind of glassy half-smile, and you know that this moment is going to be what you remember about the events that lead to the tragedy.

The guy talked for almost five and a half hours straight. He had what I guess is either a Chicago or a Detroit accent: The kind that sounds most natural filtered through a cigar.

Mostly he talked about how he was an amateur prizefighter and that he was getting pretty good at it. Short, pudgy, egotistical, in a rolling breadbox with a bad muffler and no shocks to speak of.

"Country music?" he said.

"Sure." Love those steel guitars.

Lyrics like "My girlfriend left with my pickup truck, now I'm all alone with no one to fuck". Can't get much more realistic than that. For some people.

Gimme Bach or classic rock any day. Hell, for that matter I'll take the greatest hits of the fuckin' Bee Gees first. Death before Disco, Craniotomy before Country. (We've got a sign on Colfax Avenue in Denver that says "Country Disco", and as a reasonable person, it scares the hell out of me.) At least the stereo was lousy.

"Great, how far to Toledo?" I said.

Around this time I was finally getting the idea through my brick-thick skull that this guy had a hangup about being tough. I also realized that the highway signs that should have said 80/90 East said 43. And the sun, which should have been setting behind us, was setting somewhere off the port side.

"Hey man, do you have a map?"

"Yeah."

"Can I see it?"

"Yeah, I gut a map."

"Can I See It?"

"Yeah, I gut a map."

"Where is it?" This was not getting terribly productive.

"Yeah, I gut a map. It's right here." he says while making a gun gesture with his hand and pointing to his temple.

"Well, I think we're heading North. I'm supposed to be goin' East."

"No man, you're headin' East," he says.

"But the sun is on the left. That means we're goin' North. Right?" Three years in the Boy Scouts has to be good for something.

"Look, you're here." he says, pointing to the back of his right hand. I've seen enough people from Michigan do that ridiculous mitten/map thing to know that he was pointing to the right hand the wrong way, and I'd seen enough people drive cars to know that you don't point to the back of one hand with the other at sixty-five miles an hour in a twenty-pound car. Call it an observation.

64

"O.k.," I said reassuringly.

"You're going to be here. Detroit."

"Detroit?" I said with a little doubt creeping into my voice again.

"Yeah, Detroit. Great place. I grew up there. Dis is a good ride. You'll go a long way. Dey gut dis new road dat goes direct ta Toleda, which is right there," he says, pointing again.

Yes, Virginia, this is what psychotherapy is for.

Can you say "Prozac"?

I thought you could.

He went on like this for a while and I figured that it was like a trip to the dentist. It's going to be a drag and a bit of a pain, but it isn't anything you can't survive. I'd been on Interstate 80, a road that already went directly to Toledo, but that was sort of beside the point.

Just humor him, and hope he doesn't show me his gun to prove how tough he is. Try to look impressed at all times. Keep the little Toon happy. And never get into cars with strangers. Not for candy or even transcontinental transport.

We stopped for gas and he bought me a small coffee with a Sweet 'N Low, three sugars and two creams while I got the windshield. He had to repeat the order to the girl at the drive-up window three times. I take my coffee black with one sugar, but that too was beside the point. I hadn't asked for the coffee, but I was a guest.

He got two dollars and eighty-seven cents' worth of gas; I don't know why.

We drove on for a while longer and he told me about himself. I was fascinated. My eyebrow arched, uh, archly. How bad the relations with his parents were, and how he had lost another job with another Police Benevolent Association, apparently for misrepresenting himself as a cop once too often while telemarketing for donations (and I had a feeling that there was perhaps more to it than that).

He said that he had "worked this scam in a number of different cities and it always paid good". I guess Gary, Indiana had very little sense of humor about that sort of thing.

I ran across the Time-Life Collection of Serial Killers in a used-book store recently. A bizarre compilation, in pretty questionable taste, but interesting. Biz is Biz, I guess. I looked at it but didn't buy it.

One of the Hillside Stranglers referred to some minor alteration of their Modus Operandi as "working a scam" too. Another one said that a clown can get away with murder. How comforting. Never did trust clowns.

We stopped again, for another three dollars' worth of cheap lo-lead, at a small Mom & Pop combination liquor/grocery store and gas station. They had garlic bread, toasted and stale, twelve pieces for a dollar, and he bought me some even after I declined the offer. People buying you coffee or whatever was not something I'd ever asked for on the road, but if somebody offers, it's rude to decline. Only a fool turns down free sustenance when it's needed. Don't break bread with any but a friend (duress does not count!). The North African Nomads know this.

Pretty young girl behind the counter. As I walked out the door I heard him insulting her. This guy was busy calling this scrubbed-faced, clear-eyed, innocent young girl with even white teeth, who was obviously working at the little family operation after school, a filthy (seven pejorative invective adjectives here) cunt, while her father or whoever was on the other side of the store (presumably somewhere near the shotgun). I doubted she knew the words.

I headed for the car, feeling like a character in one of those car-and-teenage-crime-spree movies. It was locked. I probably don't want to try to walk out of wherever-the-hell-this-is anyway.

He came out of the door, over a minute later, literally skipping with mirth and cackling like a character in a nineteenth-century opium nightmare. He started the car while rolling backwards. I thought for a moment that he was going to drive away with my backpacks and leave me there. He had the car in reverse and moving before he opened the back door for me.

I kept looking for the girl's father to come out and drop a shotgun blast right into the windshield. He drove out of there laughing like mad at his cleverness and her dismay, describing what had happened.

He tried to emulate the way her face fell. He had insulted her because, apparently, she deserved it for being both good-looking and sexily dressed, in knee-length cutoff overalls, boat shoes with dark blue socks and a white turtleneck with small animals on it. She had a colored plastic barrette in her straight-combed hair.

He said she also deserved it because she was obviously "a Guinea or a Rican or something." I asked him why he felt it necessary to take her apart for being something that he didn't like. What the hell, I had a psycho under glass here and I wanted to understand why and what he hated. If this was all a complex way to get around to killing me, it was going to happen or it wasn't.

I took a bit of advice from a rape-prevention class that a friend of mine attended; I humored him until another opportunity presented itself. There wasn't anything else to do, but I knew that somewhere a young, confused girl was crying.

He went on to explain to me about how all "Them People are taking over God's Country". He detailed how the Jews were taking over all the good places in the world. It was rather convoluted, and involved an American president named Franklin D. Roosenfeld.

He said that he personally knew that they were plotting to destroy the economy of the United States so they could put delis and banks on every corner, really. Turn the sacred White House into a pawnshop. They apparently called up Lucifer (on a toll-free number, or a WATTS line, presumably) and signed this pact. There is documentation, apparently.

The Fags and the Dykes and the Catholic Church are supposed to be arming too. Democrats are Communists and everybody knows Communism comes from the devil. A.C.L.U., or maybe N.A.A.C.P., is the true Number of The Beast. Right.

I'll spare you the rest of the rap, but I'm sure you get the general idea. An amazingly intricate trip that ran the gamut from the Limbaughs and McCarthys to the right reverends of limousine televangelism, and all the way over to The Grateful Dead.

Afraid America would be overrun by Americans? Feel Amerika is falling behind technologically? Vote this asshole's heros into Washington next time around. He has an idea for a new microwave oven: it seats fifty.

There is an untitled story song from a folk musician named Peter Himmelman. It used to be called "Taxi ride with a cut-rate Aryan", and this clown certainly was one. I heard the song a few weeks after this trip and had a minor case of the shakes.

When we got to Detroit he drove me around a little to show me the damage that he said was attributable to Jews and minorities, some even to women. He quoted an old redneck joke about "shooting 'Cans"

67

(Afri-cans, Mexi-cans, Puerto Ri-cans). Guided tour of a very heavy neighborhood by a Manson wannabe. The armor-plated ice cream truck plays Megadeth's greatest hits.

Detroit was in tough shape at the time and looks like it will be getting worse for a long time to come, but I can't imagine how the Radical Anti-Christ Lesbians' Alliance to be Non-White could be responsible for it. Michael Moore had tried to ask some folks why it was like this, but the answers were not directly helpful. The dirty jokes were okay, but the answers didn't help.

My copy of Robert Anton Wilson's book about the Illuminati, by the way, was given to me by this little hippie-chick in Birkenstocks and a peasant skirt, who had tried to kill it with a big two-penny nail. She pounded it through the thing's heart with a framing hammer and was busily looking for a paper shredder when I happened along.

The closed shops and abandoned buildings of downtown Detroit did look pretty rough. The prostitutes looked evil and feral, and everything looked like broken concrete or garish plastic. Abandoned want-ad sections whipped down sandy battened streets. Stripped cars sat at beheaded parking meters.

Bright motel sodium arcs in grimy parking lots. Chain hostelries for the people from other places who have come to close the city down illuminated the rats between the cracked curbing and debris in the parking lots. Busy little men with complex laptop computers and scratching pens. Men with neat hairless faces and no trace of an accent. Rubble-strewn lots around lighted high-security buildings. Cyberpunk nightmare dystopic perspective.

Of course it could have been the company I was keeping.

The American auto industry has shown that there is no love for the workers. They come from somewhere and do a job, and then they go away. It is surely an inconvenience that they need sleep and paychecks and dental plans.

"Pets or Meat" indeed.

The old standard about what's good for General Motors being good for the country could be turned around, and it looked like it had. Thank you, Mr. Reagan. Thank you, Mr. Smith. Welcome to Metropolis, Dr. Rotwang.

If this is what has happened to the grand imperial city of the American automobile industry, then something is fucking doomed. So we're never going to get the winged atomic cars they promised us back in the fifties. No flying wings, no Lucite buildings, no amazing miracles from Deus Ex Machina. Somehow we must have blown it. Maybe we just believed a lie; or a lot of them.

I don't know if it is the whole culture, or only the automobile side of it, but Detroit is certainly all done. Turn out the light when you leave.

Have you ever seen somebody whose work was their whole life have to retire? If they have nothing else to do, they die. Detroit is dying, and with it a way of living that used to be good to some people.

I was actually surprised when the feral little fuck let me out at a gas station on the fringes of Ford Avenue. Reprieve: Paroled into a nightmare he wanted me to have.

He said I "could just take route 75 over there down to Toledo and prolly get a ride by the time I got to the top of the ramp."

I walked through the other side of the attached convenience store, and he watched me go. I can still see his beady little rat's eyes behind the windshield, yellow light gleaming on the glass from the overhead lights. His recently-repaired nose looked like something you plug in at Christmas. Rudolph the red-nosed sociopath.

When I got to the other side of the store, he was sitting in his car on that side of the building. Cat and Mouse. Maybe because I was not sufficiently impressed with him. If I was lying to him somehow, I could be in deep trouble. Maybe he'd want to show me his gun after all. I got the bathroom key from the attendant and tried to wash my face awake. It had been forty-some hours and a long way over a thousand miles since sleep.

You could objectively say that I hid in there for almost twenty minutes; I'd probably agree. Maybe I'm a coward, but I'm a breathing coward.

When I came out he was gone and I returned the key. I asked the attendant how far it was to Toledo. He and the attendant security guard told me, with the expression of a cow on a passing train, that Toledo was in, huh, Ohio. The security guard undid the hammer strap on his big revolver. I reiterate, dynamite the fucking Midwest and push the coasts together.

"Gee, great. Thanks." With useful information like this, it was going to be a long night. The mist was rolling in, and the temperature had dropped thirty degrees.

It was after midnight in Detroit, but it looked okay.

Chapter 13

Foggy Night in Michigan

" What do we do if one of the big beasties out there
decides to break in,
instead of going bump in the night?"
- From Skeleton Crew, The Mist, by Stephen King

It was Midnight on a Saturday night, on some highway that I'd never heard of, walking out of Detroit. It was foggy, and I was walking South with a sign that said East.

For this I go to College?

Tell me again; why I do this stupid shit?

At around three thirty I was sitting in the breakdown lane, barely illuminated by the sodium arc lights from a Coca Cola distributor, modifying the back of my cardboard sign with a red ball point pen I found in my bag.

I got a little annoyed at the sound of all the big thyroidal V-eight engines and large comfortable cars not even slowing down to acknowledge me. Imagining the soft clean warm upholstery, the machine made brocade of mass-produced American comfort on wheels, blissfully tuned to digital quad stereo as I hiked though the impenetrable Michigan mist with my feet stinking and my jeans sticking to my butt.

I was in the process of standing up, throwing my sign on the ground and preparing to yell a little, purely for therapeutic purposes, when a Michigan State Police cruiser, going by in the second lane, locked up its brakes and slid in front of me in a controlled four wheel slide. He turned on his bubble lights and backed around me so that I was in front of him.

So much for finding a safe place for primal scream therapy.

The driver had all of his lights on me (including high beams and both spot lights). So I put my packs down and stepped two feet to the side while keeping my hands in very plain sight. I opened my jacket with the tips of my fingers, just like on television.

The driver got out of the car and asked me what I was doing. He was so far back that he had to shout a couple of times and turn off

70

his quickly ululating siren. I bent carefully, picked up my sign and pointed at it, smiling and nodding reassuringly, while trying to keep from laughing. The answer seemed pretty obvious to me but then I have been told that I am overly perceptive at times. I mimed thumbing.

After running a check on three of the picture id's in my wallet and looking at the phone card, credit cards (way over the limit and due to expire without benefit of clergy very soon, but very good for effective external proof of stability), student id's for the past few years and a copy of the Bill of Rights (That particular item got a scowl and a raised eyebrow. Might be potentially seditious and subversive material: you never know what the hell somebody will do with one of those things).

He asked me who I was, as though I, maybe, had never read my identification cards. (Irony is not a country in the Middle East!) This also seemed pretty evident, but since police have to deal with all sorts of people, and only a few people are willing to take jobs where people shoot at you, I explained that I was hitchhiking to school because it was the only mode of transportation that I could afford. His partner grunted symbolically, he had heard of this kind of thing.

After patting me down, and missing the emergency lock-blade I was carrying, they put my bags in the trunk and drove me to the next exit. The Sergeant driving told me that there was a truck-stop about two miles inland. He said I'd be able to get a ride from there.

Hardcore interstate travelers, especially those with a little road-burn, have a bias against going "inland." There's no telling if the local police lie in wait for you at the bottom of the exit ramp, or whether the roads will be unnavigable close after all those broadband miles of multi-lane interstate travel.

About four miles inland there was an airport. Now, my father, as I've mentioned, has been a truck driver for thirty years, and the father of an ex-girlfriend of mine was an airline pilot. I know, on an intellectual and philosophical level, there is a little similarity between the two professions. I was not in any mood for intellectual or philosophical bullshit.

While hiking back out I noticed, in an open portion of fog, that there was a house lot that seemed to be abandoned and pretty isolated. A foundation and a couple of outbuildings, but that's it.

The woods were pretty dense in there and I figured that a little sleep would keep me from making any more mistakes like I had made outside of Chicago. And the fish weren't biting anyway.

It was a good place, well screened from the road by scrub bushes, mist and the thickness of the forest. After spending the last few years in Colorado, the fog was as much a treat as an annoyance. I must have looked like one of Diane Fosse's friends, even if I was getting damp. I was tired enough to sleep in the toy section of K mart on Christmas Eve.

All I could think about that related to the locale was that old Hemingway story "Up In Michigan" and the fact that there are supposed to be bears in this state. The internal brain reference guide says "Watch out for bears and people with wounded noses": okay, I can deal with that. If Roger Smith shows up, run like hell.

A forest ranger in Colorado once told me that a bear looks at a tent the way a marijuana smoker looks at a Snickers wrapper. Fortunately, I didn't have a tent.

I slept three hours on a bed of rich brown duff and small leafy emerald green plants canopied in elegant style by several tall pine trees.

I dreamt a fairytale of the old forests of Europe, of the days before the kingdoms and the wolf hunts. A dream of sweet little gingerbread cabins in the deep everwood, the smell of woodsmoke and baking bread. Painted windowboxes full of flowers, pine needle carpet, and a feeling of well-being.

The smell of bread was real and came from a cabin out of sight in the woods and mist.

When I got up the fog was a thick, odd, stuff whose equal I have seen in Boston only once. I am told that the fog is similar in Salisbury Plain, around Stonehenge, on certain days of the year. It was weird stuff, like memories, that came in different densities as you walked through, oddly thick and sparse in alternating spaces, seeming to absorb all sound and light. It would be clear for a few feet and then so thick that you literally could not see the ground under your feet.

Five thirty, or so on a foggy Michigan morning, and somebody has bread in the oven. I'm waking up in an elfish canopy bed, doing the soldier's field check: Legs, arms, knife, (no gun), lighter, watch, smokes, no immediate danger present: operating within normal parameters. Cool. Systems are GO.

72

When I was seventeen there was a girl I was seeing. We used to go to school together and spend hours at a time on the phone. She quit during her junior year and got a job at an all night restaurant a few towns over.

I used to wait until I heard my father snoring just right and then I'd roll the car out of the driveway and start the motor down at the bottom of the hill.

One night I went to see her at work, and the place was deserted except for us and the old Curandero cook. We talked and smoked and drank bad coffee together. We spoke of cabbages and kings, and the truths behind things. We spoke of her impending marriage to some guy named Fred, and the baby that would be there soon.

When I drove home the fog was as thick and heavy as the goose-down quilt at my grandmother's house. It too blocked all sound and light.

In my first car, that sweet old Chevelle, the radio hardly ever worked. I didn't see any other moving vehicles or signs of life for the fifteen miles of the trip home, and I began to think about what it would be like if the whole world had just gone away. What if it was like this forever. As if there was nobody else alive or awake in the whole world.

I got almost home, and then turned around and headed for the highway to see if there were, in fact, any other people out there anywhere.

Twenty miles later I saw a tractor-trailer and a couple of cars out on the highway. When their headlights came into view, my radio came back on. I wonder if, just perhaps I slipped a little mental cog for that half hour, or whether the world took an extra coffee break when almost nobody was looking. I'd like to pass it off, at least to myself, as the imagination of a teenager who read too much fiction.

I'd be able to if my watch hadn't been half an hour fast the next day.

It was as foggy as that night out here and the damned fools in their big warm cars had their heaters and radios on. I just know they did.

I felt just as invisible as I had that night, and I honestly wondered if maybe I was walking on a road that was really somewhere else. Come on out Mr. Serling, the game's over.

If the banquet tables of Tolkien's forest elves had appeared off to the side of the breakdown lane I'd have probably joined them. I certainly wouldn't have been surprised in the slightest to see anything but a human out there.

Can you imagine being invisible? When I was in junior high I fantasized about it so that I could slip into the girl's locker room (surprise!). After that I drove a succession of vaguely illegal cars. I never imagined that being unseen could ever be a problem.

Ralph Ellison was right. Being invisible, a nonentity might just be the hardest thing of all to deal with. You could learn to fly or just sit down and cease to be and not have anybody to tell about it.

It's a comforting anonymity in a lot of ways, but it's certainly a long way from a flush toilet. Woody Allen asks if the afterlife is open at this hour and if you can get there by cab from mid-town. I can tell him from personal experience that the other places in the world never close and you can get there at almost any hour from anywhere. The question is do you want to?

At seven thirty I was stopped by another state trooper, this one about nineteen years old. This time in a Camaro "interceptor"; a fast car for catching other fast cars. Walking in the fog was still like being wrapped in cotton, I don't know how he even saw me. I looked at my shoes to see if they had been caught on police radar.

We went through the same routine as I had with the other one the night before. When he got done running my identification he asked me why I was not walking on the bike path that had literally materialized on command out of the fog about twenty feet to the side of the road.
I explained the mechanics of hitchhiking to him and asked him about his car.

After ten minutes of careful discussion, so as not to boast of any illegalities performed while under the influence of youth (by either of us), we talked about different fast cars we had both owned. He left me to get back to the business at hand. He seemed so delighted that I thought so much of his car that he took off with all his lights going and his tires screeching. I was impressed, really. At least he was a human being. I think.

A little later an exit ramp appeared out of the fog and I decided that some breakfast was in order. I don't remember the name of the town, if I ever knew it, and I can honestly say that I could care less. My feet hurt and my frustration level was very high.

I walked into town and had toast, coffee, and an egg that tasted as if it had been cooked in WD40, for about two bucks, at a generic diner on a generic corner. It had the feel of all the breakfast joints in small towns where the real politics is done.

This must have been the real people's day off. It looked like a gathering of television sit-com extras. The place was singularly unimpressive and I don't think that anyone even noticed I was there. They must have been waiting for somebody to dub the laugh track to punctuate their best lines.

I had a brief conversation with a kid who said he drove Stock Cars out at one of the local tracks when he could afford it. Lately his girlfriend had lost her food stamps and was expecting another kid so he could not afford to go racing. He sounded bitter about everything but his car. "Getting pregnant again, what a dirty trick!"

When I got through I walked to the road and started at it again. I saw the same police officer heading the other way on the highway and he waved to me and flashed his lights. I waved back.

I remember this guy, John, from my hometown, who used to sit in the parking lot at the edge of town in the black Pontiac he'd built out of about five different cars. Late at night he'd be sitting there, listening to music or just the sound of his motor; four hundred and fifty five cubic inches of highly tuned Detroit Iron loping along on a full race cam. Just like in the Bruce Springsteen songs. I wondered what he was thinking as he smoked his Winstons and weed and drank his Miller Beers.

I wondered a lot about the mystery of the road in the days when I was waiting to get my driver's license. I knew, by heart, all the car stories that anybody told.

I knew about how the street racers used to meet at that diner down on Route 1 in Saugus, back in the early sixties. How so and so's Mom was so cool because she got him an Offenhauser manifold and an Isky cam for his Flathead.

And how the State Police had a '55 Nomad with a 451 Lincoln motor that they'd built in a special shop down in Boston. The kids called it "The Grey Ghost" and it was primer and red lead with flames sketched on the rocker panels next to the Lake side-pipes. If you didn't shut it down by the time you were on the other side of the stoplight by the Esso station bridge, the Ghost would get you. Full uniformed state trooper in the most badass car on the road. Hardcore. Shut you down just like Mitchum in Thunder Road.

I remember a guy named Steve who blew a corner out on the road near Danvers State Mental Hospital when I was in High School. His cherry red ragtop Mustang wrapped itself around a tree. The tree was an ancient dead oak or maple that had gone rotten at the core and been filled with bricks to keep it standing. The tree had died and not been taken down, and they had to take his car off of it the way you take tin foil from leftovers. A few days after the wake we cut it down and dragged it into town behind a car. Cut it loose in front of the Town Hall.

Some time after eleven I was stopped by another police officer in the same blue Camaro Interceptor. The shift must have changed, and I was feeling like a curious artifact.

He asked me the same questions and I gave him the same answers. I heard the dispatcher explain, very slowly, the concept of hitchhiking to him on the radio. He told me that I had to walk on the bike path and I explained and protested that I was trying to get out of here as fast as I could. He told me that if he had nothing better to do at the end of his shift he would come back and arrest me for vagrancy. Then he told me, foolishly, when his shift ended.

I figured that I'd be spending the latter part of the goddamned afternoon hiding behind a bush, like a comedic fugitive. If I couldn't get a ride.

Why can't there be The Ride? That perfect ride that gives just the right amount of physical and mental transport. Especially when you really want it. I dreamt of an electric painted school bus with the word "FURTHUR" painted on the front.

I dreamt, as I walked my tired wet feet further into my new shoes, of the perfect ride. I dreamt the blonde girl from Santana's (69)Woodstock set. The one with the steel rimmed glasses and that awe-filled, perfect smile. My tantric imaginary friend. Moves like Tina Weymouth. A sleek '69 Impala or Caddy with a good stereo, a mood like a gram of hash, and thou. Ahh, my Love, why hast thou forsaken me? How can you be anywhere else?

When I was a kid, the police were older than I was. They were older than everyone but the Old Folks. Big old Italian or Irish Guys with graying dark hair, sad, kind eyes and a bit of a paunch. They were like some benevolent species of uncles, perhaps from the same branch of the family as Santa Claus. One of them once told me, after catching me driving around at three in the morning at the age of sixteen, how it worked.

"Kid," he said, making me feel like Arlo Guthrie, "There's three kinds of people around at this time of the night; Good Guys, Bad Guys, and Dumb-fucks who don't know any better. What the hell are you?"

It was a classic bit, and I knew he'd been polishing it up and saving it for occasions just like this, so I paid attention. I take it out and think about it now and then. I tend to fall somewhere on the benevolent side of dumb-fuck most of the time. I'm often up at that hour, but I don't go out much.

Hiding behind a bush on a Michigan Highway from a bored cop, younger than myself, with nothing better to do than give me a hard time?

Right. If I were a Bad Guy it would make sense. He didn't want me doing what I was doing in his state, or at least on his road, and neither did I.

The natural best way to handle this would have been the way those old cops of my childhood would have. Figure out what you are dealing with and act accordingly. Toss me out of the damned state and give me a lecture on my own stupidity. Works better, and makes the point more clearly, than any civil charge you can think of.

I know one lady, who was a straight Road Person at the time, back in the seventies, when it was safe. She got caught hitching in Pennsylvania, and instead of being booked, was relayed, patrol zone to patrol zone, across the whole state. The down side was that they took her all the way to her folks' house in a nice, upscale, Philadelphia neighborhood, and explained the whole thing to her parents.

When Peach Fuzz left I felt invisible again, and that wasn't better. I sat down and modified my sign some more. I was on the point of wanting to lunge in front of the cars to at least get some confirmation that they, in fact, could see me.

The sign, here in front of me as I write this, says:

Toledo, Please
HI!
This road: 11 hours
I AM NOT DANGEROUS!

77

It is written in red ink because that is all that I had at the time. It has the previously mentioned "Opus" on the other side with the word "East". Below that is the word "Vermont" with a peace symbol drawn through the "O".

I could probably been picked up easier if I'd had a bloody machete in one hand and a sign in the other with a smiley face reading "Just killed my family". At least the dumb bastards would have some context for what the hell I was doing.

At Four O'clock I was three miles from Luna Pier, on the outskirts of Toledo when I got a lift from a guy in a pickup with Ohio plates. It was near the end of the peach-fuzz cop's shift and I was so angry and tired and nervous about getting busted on a stupid charge, that I couldn't even remember the gentleman's name. He told me, by way of apology for Michigan, about himself and some of the cultural bias that I was facing up in Michigan.

He told me that they had only heard about hitchhikers in Michigan, and those mostly on the news after a murder. Even if it wasn't related to the murder, it was part of the standard litany of horrors. He said that people were somewhat difficult about things that were "different" and told me that the fact that he was black, and had married a white woman made it necessary for him to leave the job he had been at for eighteen years (a large, reputable company too) and live down in Ohio.

The racism, resentment, or whatever it is that makes people weird about variety, and diversity seemed to stop at the Ohio line. Interracial marriage? They are both human, the important question should be "Do they love each other?" or "Are they Good to/for each other?" Hate, despite what some people will tell you, is NOT a "Family Value".

He stopped for gas and bought lottery tickets and cigarettes. One of his tickets won. Hit for five dollars, and he gave one to me. Said you should all ways share good luck. I tried to decline politely and he told me not to be an idiot. Besides, he said, one of the other tickets had won twenty bucks.

I thanked him and washed the windshield while he pumped the gas. The four losing tickets he'd just scratched were face down on the seat.

I got some Granola bars and a bottle of apple juice and tried to remember that humanity was still tolerable in some places.

From looking at my maps now, I can see that he went ten miles out of his way to drop me at the exit five truck-stop back on I-80. As I got out of the truck he thanked me for giving him someone to talk to. (Sir, Thank You. You are truly a Gentleman.)

It was nearly sunset on Toledo. Not the Detroit kind of sunset, just almost nightfall. It was sunny and I lay down on thick grass, in the shade of a rock maple, next to the highway overpass for Exit Five and began to relax for the first time since Iowa.

It had taken me twenty-four hours to get from Denver to Chicago and another twenty four to get from there to Toledo, Ohio. So much for a hitchhiking land speed record. I thought about Henry sitting in his truck in that rest area on the other side of Chicago. I guess this was Somebody-Up-There's way of telling me that maybe I shouldn't have left him alone.

Walking over the back side of the ramp and into the back lot of the "Red Ball" truck-stop was a little trickier than I thought it would be, and I had to rescue a shoe that the mud almost decided to keep.

When I got my feet rinsed off and some more clean socks on I went into the diner. Always carry a plastic bag for dirty socks on long hikes, trust me.

I washed up and shaved in the civilian restroom, completely forgetting that these places have showers for the Drivers. Access is tighter the further East you happen to be I can pass for, and usually am mistaken for a Driver in most truck stops. The trick is to look like either an urban mountain man or a suburban cowboy. If I'd thought of it, I'd have taken a shower as well.

I went into the restaurant and sat on the edge of the "Drivers only" section with my backpacks on the other side of the booth. The coffee was both wonderful and crucial at that point, and the luxury of a scoop of strawberry ice cream was unimaginably decadent.

You have to do nice things for yourself periodically. You'd be surprised how little it takes.

Along with showers, these places have other essentials for road people, starchy food, television rooms and video games and collect or calling card phones at the tables. The trick to being able to use these luxuries is to look like you belong there. I called my father to let him know how far I'd come. At least I think it was my father I called. It was a long day.

I also called Maryann, my roommate in Denver, and checked on how she was doing. About the same, she said, and would it be all right if her ex-boyfriend slept on my futon while he was helping to remodel one of the bedrooms. Sure, as he's probably been sleeping on it for a couple of days already.

I sat for as long as I could justify it to myself, nearly an hour and a half. This is not time as measured when you are at work or school; it's not even measured the way time is measured in your living room. The intervals are flexible. It was how much I needed, and I remembered to tip 15%, because I was not likely to be the only guy to come through here with a backpack.

Crossroads waitresses see all the misfortunes that befall travelers. Every boat on the blacktop sea washes up here eventually.

I once nursed a bottomless cup of coffee, at a truck-stop out near Ogalalla, for eleven hours while waiting for a Western Union Money Order, but that story is for another day.

I walked across the street to the other truck stop.

Chapter 14

Toledo to New York

"When I was back there in seminary school there was a person
there who put forth the preposition that you could
petition the lord with prayer.
Petition the Lord with prayer...
Petition the Lord with prayer....
YOU CANNOT PETITION THE LORD WITH PRAYER!!"
- from Soft Parade, by Jim Morrison

"Confucius does his crossword with a pen"
- from Happy Phantom by Tori Amos

I stood at the bottom of the entrance ramp for about an hour, afraid even to try slipping around the back of the tolls at their top. I also have to admit that I was in no mood for any more walking at the time, or to describe and explain the peculiar activity of hitchhiking to any more people in Uniforms, even if it was a different State.

A lot of people beeped and waved at me and I was happy about it for a change. I'm not sure why people do that, must pass for wit somewhere, but it seems unusually cruel; but I was just glad to be seen.

There was a lady I used to know, whose husband beat her. She said that sometimes it's good to just be able to know that somebody is paying attention. Always seemed like a tough way to know you are real, to have confirmation of your existence.

There are millions of different kinds of pain in the world, usually cumulative, subtle offenses against the spirit or the mind, often inflicted with transcendent patience and surgical-laser precision by people with nothing better to do. But the victims of that kind of torture will usually tell you that they at least know someone is paying attention.

A truck pulled up to the light going into the truck stop I'd just been in. The driver pounded on his door as he pulled through the light and yelled "Come on man." I followed the truck onto the lot and into the garage. He had a flat tire on his inside rear trailer dual. I figured "what the hell." Either I'd end up getting a couple of bucks for helping him change the tire or I'd get a ride to somewhere East.

The Driver, was a six foot three black guy named Billy, and the Mechanic was singularly unhelpful to him until I caught up. The Mechanic kept asking me the relevant details of what kind of new tire and mud flap did we want. That's what racial bias looks like some places.

I hang around with some pretty peaceful folks. I'd forgotten that this kind of crap still happened as part of doing your day's work, but ignorance is no excuse. The tire got changed in about half an hour and we got the hell out of there.

We drove through the night, highballing, listening to the CB radio and his stash of seventies funk and soul tapes.

Parliament/Funkadelics and old flash-dressed Barry White were way too commercial for Billy's collection, and it was a real learning experience. Later, after discussing, in shouted short sentences, the riots in Los Angeles, we listened to some of his Martin Luther King tapes. Billy's tape collection was pretty diverse, even had some Merle Haggard in there.

There is a thing that truckers all do with their radios. They tend to crank the balance knob over to the right a bit so that the sound is balanced over the noise of the engine. The mix on most of this stuff was probably done in very primitive early stereo, and the audience sounds on Dr. King's speeches are all on the right side channel.

But we were flying through the darkness as fast as that truck would go.

In Dr. King's "Knock on The Door" sermon (which we listened to twice) there is the high, nasal voice of a young man who keeps saying "That's right" very precisely and emphatically, in the manner of so many young black men back then, who, in proving that thy were the equal of anyone else, became the best mannered, intelligent and articulate people around.

Now you can't even publish the names of kids who kill kids, or even the ones who carry guns in school. You can't even publish the names of their parents and hope peer pressure will even it all out. That shit wouldn't fly with Dr. King or Malcolm X, but then, where are they now?

I could picture this nasal guy in the crowd as Dr. King spoke: Young and wiry, in a narrow tie suit, white shirt, maybe wearing one of those little hats (I don't know what they are called, or why I was picturing a Muslim hat at a Christian speech) that the Black Muslims wore. I could see the guy's thin face in my head, short hair and those pointy cornered birth control glasses that everyone wore in the sixties. Despite the peace and truth and goodness of Dr. King's words, I wanted to punch that little guy. "That's right", his voice was killing me.

We hit the Throgs Neck Expressway into New York early in the morning after highballing through the night.

So, What's a Throg? If this is the damned neck....

The traffic was terrible and I really should have gotten off at the point where route 90 splits off of 80 in western Pennsylvania. I had a ride into New York and, damn it, I wasn't about to get out and walk through the middle of Pennsylvania. I don't care if I get to see steel towns and the Amish out for a buggy ride; I want to reach the East. In Western States terms, the distance from New York to Boston is negligible; 300 miles was what I'd done that first afternoon, but I'd been off the East Coast for a long time.

Now, the Throgs Neck is not to believed if you've never been there. You go from reasonably open road back in Pennsylvania, to slightly more congested as you cross that bottom triangle of New York, to totally congested as you get near The City: to totally congested and on-going construction when you're there.

Not a lot of fun. The traffic moves at about five miles an hour and the smell is terrible; refried hydrocarbons, rotting buildings and the decomposing river are only part of it. The place badly needs to be hosed down.

The CB Radio is not the rescue and communication tool that it is in the West or the North. In New York it is a stage for every idiot who wants to have a captive audience. You have to listen to it just to figure out what lane you should be in to avoid the construction, but you don't have to like it.

I spent some time being mystified as to why there were so many jerks trying to over-key drivers trying to do their jobs. I also spent some time trying to figure out what the point of some of this silliness was. Like cities: why bother?

There is a whole world of CB people out there. Similar to computer bulletin board users and ham radio folks in many ways. Like

83

Internet discussion lists these days. Many of them are just folks who use the thing as a tool to do their jobs.

Another segment of the community got into the things back in the seventies when C.W. McCall did the song "Convoy." (Many truckers are still waiting to catch McCall in a dark alley for that) These "civilians" Have been adding power mikes, signal boosters and massive antennas to their powerful home base-stations, as their pension checks or whatever income they have allows, for years. Many of them seem to spend the day in front of the radio with a bottle and an attitude. Many of the truckers have high-powered set ups too.

Billy was using an echo box on his microphone line that made his voice come across the radio like the rolling voice of God in an old movie. Other guys used different noise-makers that would simulate Model-T horns or lion roars.

One of the strangest things I have ever heard on the radio was a sound like a woman having an orgasm, a very satisfying orgasm, (at top volume) followed immediately by the sound of a dog barking. A big dog, like a Great Dane or something. A happy "thanks for the steak" bark. The fertile mind imagines many strange things. I thought that it was an excerpt from someone's very strange private life being broadcast.

It was not until much later that I learned about the sound boxes. They apparently sell for around fifty dollars apiece, so somebody out there had dropped about a hundred bucks, to provide the fertile minds of the world something weird to ponder.

Billy said that he had to do one stop and then he would drop me off at a truck-stop where I could surely get a ride North to Boston.

My family has been in the trucking business since at least my great-grandfather's time. We still have the medal and ribbon from when he won first prize in the 1906 Labor Day parade for best horse and freight wagon.

I'd spent a lot of my childhood around trucks. The first poem I ever wrote, or so my grandmother tells me, was about trucks. (I was a weird kid, O.K.?) They were, from a Freudian perspective, probably symbolically representative of my father and adulthood, power through mobility, or some such bullshit.

The opportunity to run freight around New York is a chance to experience something that I'd never had, and because I've chosen not to take up that life, not one that I'm ever likely to have again. So I didn't mind when that one stop at the Postal Annex in Yonkers turned into another stop at a Sanyo distributor in mid-town.

I didn't even mind when that one turned into a trip to an auto parts distributor in Queens and that into a hose manufacturer in Brooklyn. Though I will offer a word of advice; never try to move a pallet of sparkplugs without a forklift or dolly, and never leave a pallet of sparkplugs unattended on a New York Street.

I have been to New York a couple of times. Mostly just going down to look at places that I'd read about, and seeing the touristy things that I could find from Downtown.

When I lived near Boston, I would take the old Eastern shuttle down every year or two after I got out of High school. The Empire State Building, Statue of Liberty, The Met, The Museums of Modern Art and Natural History, Radio City. The famous places that even Boston can't top. I even went down for New Year's Eve one year. The fare was around twenty dollars, and it was pretty cool.

My experience has told me (as you might guess) that I don't want to spend much time anywhere near the place. The tourist stuff and the museums were great, but I'd never felt the real attraction of The Big City. I had a chance to look at the graffiti on the bottom of the Brooklyn Bridge. The glorious tasks of engineering and the Walt Whitman poem did not jibe with the gang tags and all the swears that Holden Caulfield had wanted to rub out.

There was one that might have been art: an old console television, with aerial, rendered in subtle pastel spray-bomb, with "TV Fuddlehead" written under it. A tip of the hat to the highly stylized Modern Art U.P.A cartoons of the fifties.

The swears made me think of Lenny Bruce and Holden Caulfield, and that bastard who shot John Lennon sitting down to read Catcher In The Rye. The television made me think of a skinny little punk rock girl who used to work in a cafe in Boulder. She had a tattoo of a television just like that on her upper arm. She said she thought, from time to time, about adding the word "Mother" to it.

The skyline looks nice in pictures but, who in their right mind would really want to live here when there is land practically free in the mountains of Colorado and Wyoming? (yea, Dumb question. Besides, you wouldn't like it anyway. Stay home. Please, Stay home. There are lions and bears and Indians and stuff: Stay the fuck home! Please.)

When we got to the place where Billy was to do his last delivery and pick up, all the guys who worked there forgot how to speak English and somehow, consequently, how to unload a truck. I need to ask a linguist about that.

It took us over an hour to get the awkward metal racks off of the truck without any kind of dolly. As we were closing the doors the foreman came out, remembering his English long enough to tell us that we needed to load several dozen seven foot high by four foot wide rolls of reinforced hose. It was late afternoon and we didn't know anything about doing a pickup as well.

We both sat down and lit up. Suddenly his crew reappeared and remembered how to speak the language. They loaded half the truck very quickly and rather badly (freight needs to be stacked properly in a truck or it will waste space, bounce around and break). I'll give them this: they were enthusiastic. We loaded the other half and got almost twice as much in.

It was four-thirty in the afternoon and I was pretty tired of this nonsense. I wanted to go home and take a shower and wake up in a week. Billy, on the other hand, decided that he wanted to find some pot.

Hold it! Time out!!

Gotta break the Brechtian fourth wall again, for a second, just like Bugs Bunny and Daffy Duck used to do.

Excuse me for a second here, Dear Reader, but: At the moment I am a Full Time College Student. The pay is lousy, but they tell me there is a great future in it.

However, due to sworn and sacred oaths, sacrosanct preclusions, and contractual obligations that are imposed upon me by my student loan agreements, The Federal Government, and its litigious little minions, I can be prosecuted under a couple of different provisions of the RICO act for "dealing with, having knowledge of, possessing, using, distributing or having ever bloody well heard anything explicit about anything that may ever be considered a "controlled substance".

The penalties, as I understand them, include the loss of further student loan eligibility (hence my living and continuation of my mortgaged future), unreasonable search and seizure of my possessions (which could be embarrassing, as I own, such embarrassing goodies as a signed first edition of Paradise Alley, written by Sylvester Stallone), as well as leading to undignified conversations with armed and upset DEA and FBI folks at ludicrously early hours of the morning.

Consider how my conversations with Law Enforcement Minions go and cut me some slack, please. So, since there is already no significant Sex or Rock & Roll in this story, please assume that I made up the following couple of paragraphs in the interest of literary flavoring and exotic spice or something. O.K.? Thanks.

We now return you to your regularly scheduled reading, already in progress.

Billy asked the hippest looking kid on the loading dock where a person might locate the substance in question. The kid told him to go up to the corner grocery store and ask the old dude behind the counter.

Needless to say, we must have looked like rejects from the Hill Street Blues undercover squad. A heavy-set white guy in jeans and a dress shirt worn loose, over a tee shirt with an architectural motif, and a black guy in jeans, tee-shirt, cowboy boots and a black bandanna. Cops or idiots.

When Billy started asking the old dude about "smoke" the guy proudly displayed his cigarette rack and gold tooth, then he held a number of different brands up beside his face while talking a mile a minute in a combination of Persian, English and Portuguese. He looked like a bad television commercial waiting to happen. Maybe he though one of us was really a hidden camera. ABSCAM's funniest home videos. We went back and found the kid.

The kid and Billy went to the place with the pot. The guy behind the counter showed the kid his cigarettes for a while and they left. Maybe the guy thought we had something on him. Billy bought the kid a Coke and had him wait there while he went back and got the truck.

He was getting a little impatient, and more than a little insulted to be suspected of being a cop, so he came back and parked the truck directly in front of the store.

Brooklyn is all kinds of close together and a tractor-trailer takes up an awful lot of room. It took them close to forty minutes to come back and the storeowner came out and glowered at me sitting in the passenger seat for a while. I went in and bought a pack of generic cigarettes.

When they got back we sat in the truck and smoked for a while. I didn't know you could get Jamaican pot in the states anymore. Billy was amazed that he was able to buy it right over the counter at the health food store out of one of those gallon herb jars. I did not smoke very much of it because the catnip they sold him had a little too much pot in it for me. (catnip produces a nice mellow high, while pot messes me up entirely- like I needed that at the moment?) It took the edge off a little.

Anyway, Billy dropped me off at what had to be the grungiest, most run down truck-stop that I've ever heard of. He said he was sorry he couldn't get me closer to where I was going. He apologized profusely for the truck-stop. The place was amazing; almost comedically grimy.

The lot chatter on the CB was a trip, to say the least. Talk of drugs and things illegal are forbidden by the FCC and I had always figured that it was just a breach of ethics to discuss them openly. So I'm a little naive.

Ol' Billy didn't have any luck getting me a ride either. I wasn't female, or exactly another driver, so I was out of luck. He parked, and we thought about it for a while. I guess I should have lied and told him I was a Driver. At one point I saw a pudgy naked man in cowboy boots and hat carry a naked woman out of his truck and drop her into a mud puddle. It looked like he was carrying a mannequin.

I stood in front of the diner for about two hours and then stood in front of an Exxon station slightly closer to the highway for a while more. Not enough room to get a good walk going, nowhere for a truck to stop.

I was experiencing the same invisibility that I had encountered in Michigan the previous day, and I was not happy about it. I asked a kid in the gas station how likely I was to get a ride out of here soon. Where was a good place to stand. He did not even look up from doing his shift sheet and said "Nobody EVER gets out of here, Man."

Excuse the naivete again here folks, but I was thinking of New Jersey, you know, where Springsteen types drive late sixties muscle cars because they are a little alienated. Maybe I was thinking of Jersey suburbanites, a little bland, and maybe as confusing as New Yorkers seem to find them, I did not expect this kind of nihilistic bullshit philosophy at all. I went back and stood in front of the truck-stop for a while longer.

I had another sign that my roommate had made me but I had barely used. It depicted Opus lying down with the word "Boston" next to him. I folded it so that Opus wouldn't show (and so people wouldn't get the wrong idea.) I stood there for another hour or so. The only person who paid me any attention was a prostitute who wanted to bum a cigarette. To actually be acknowledged, I gave her two.

Eventually, I walked out of there. The first thing I had to cross was the little two-lane drawbridge near the gas station. The attendant never looked up.

The bridge overhead was this heavy black iron affair that was totally dwarfed by what my maps tell me is, I think, the "Tappan Zee" bridge. I'm not really sure, and I don't want to go back and look. It was a very high, big, black bridge. It spanned an enormous distance. It was not on my path so I did not think about it for more than a few minutes.

I walked through the maze of on and off ramps thinking that it looked vaguely like the same interchange depicted in an old black light Fabulous Furry Freak brothers poster that one of my uncles had when I was a kid. Midnight Rider, a classic.

I walked up over the edge of a couple of off ramps and sidled right up along side of the tollbooth to get on the Jersey Turnpike. I walked around behind the little shack that the toll takers must use as an office or something and sat down beside a small tree next to where they park their cars.

I'd been awake for about four days. The last sleep had been a couple of hours in the moist green forests of Michigan, over thirty hours before, and that doesn't count here anyway.

This is Jersey, nothing counts. Nobody gets out of here, man. All I could think of was:

1) Hitchhiking is very illegal in Jersey, has been since the Depression so the hobos couldn't get to the nice vacation spots upstate.

2) Interstate 95 goes through Boston and right past my old high school. If I could do that too, I'd be home soon. I could borrow something with a motor, and go from there.

3)   This was I-95.

4)   I could see no sign to indicate North from where I was, and I'd gotten a little turned around on all those ramps.

5)   East. I'm out of East. Gotta go North now.

      Of these problems, only the last really troubled me. It was a slightly overcast night so the North Star was not visible. No moss grows on the freeway. I'd taken my compass out of my backpack before I left home, because I figured I wouldn't need it.

      The moon was at her highest point of the night and I had made the journey to the East, not the East of peaceful heaven perhaps, and certainly not The East of my own enlightenment. I had gone East and run out of land, so I must be close to the end of the journey.

      By a process which was, at that time, slightly more difficult than taking Pi to it's eighty seventh place without a scratch pad, I was able to remember that the Moon was over the tropic of Capricorn this time of year. So the moon would be slightly to the south. Tropic of Cancer?

      Henry Miller said " this is not a book, it is a prolonged insult, a gobbous spit in the face of truth beauty, Art", etc... He must have been to Jersey once himself. After double-checking my figures a couple of times and a coin toss, I started off (hopefully) North.

      I'd made about four miles when a young Indian guy in a Lincoln Towncar limo picked me up. Always trust the moon. I know that I must have looked bad, and I'm sure that I smelled worse, but if he was willing to pick me up, I sure wasn't going to turn down a ride.

      He dropped me at the entrance to the Lincoln Tunnel. Despite the offer, I was in no shape to arrive Downtown in a limo. It would have given me a perverse kind of joy to arrive with all of twenty cents in my pocket, in Manhattan, in a limo. Maybe it would make any future successes that much more significant, but I had little desire for the grand entrance to The City. In point of fact, I had no desire for any city at all. What next?

      Just keep moving. The trick to survival is to just keep moving.

Chapter 15

The City

"I know that despite all the warnings against hitchhikers
I can step to the highway, thumb for a ride and
in a few minutes a car or a truck will stop
and someone will say, 'Climb in, Mac- how far you going?'"
- from "This I Believe", by Robert A. Heinlein

I walked along for a couple of hours thinking about all the stories I'd read and heard about the road I was on. Like seeing the backsides of famous Los Angeles set locations in Mike Jittlov's "The Wizard of Speed and Time". I kept coming back to the part of Stephen King's novel "The Stand", where a couple of survivors of biological holocaust have to crawl out of town via the Lincoln tunnel.

Everyone talks about New York as if it were all downtown, bright laser cannon Klieg lights over the well known skyline, shiny city club openings and celebrities: nobody talks about the Dresden rubble of The Bronx. New York is the great metropolis of the western world. It is supposed to be the place where ART happens. It is supposed to be a golden city, a great shining heaven; that magic realm where the famous have to go.

New York, like all the great cities of the world, for all travelers, is a fucking nuisance. It is an inconvenience on a scale unimaginable elsewhere. It smells bad, full of dangerous people who would happily kill you, in randomly brutal and graphic ways, for any commodity they might covet: anything of value, pocket change, Real Estate, cigarettes, dreams, internal organs, something you stole from somebody else, your soul. Anything at all. There are people who have made an art form of ultra-violence, and there are those who like to watch. Some of both groups wear suits.

I suppose if it's your place, your indigenous habitat, you might feel differently about it or you wouldn't be there. But like the rest of the cities of the industrial East, they have the smell of death upon them. At least for me.

The halls of old Harvard up in Boston have a genteel mummification, and ghosts whose secrets you can necromance away.

91

In the old places you can see a bit of how people lived, and comprehend the things they did in life.

This is a stone wall, abandoned to the forest by its makers who went West for gold in the middle of the last century. This is a poem made by a fragile woman who never had to leave the house. This is the house the famous man lived in. This is a family of ten that died during the influenza. That stone memorial is to the men who held the British at bay during the war that is more fondly remembered than the recent ones. Beautiful and educational, but still the things of death.

New York's walls are police tape and gutters filled with viscera. The big houses are separated from the common folks by security systems and the unfathomable, unspanable gulf of massive new corporate wealth, unknown manners and genteel old family money.

I was wondering about how long it would take Mother Nature to reclaim all of this after it all falls apart, and it will someday, as all cities seem to, when a family of rabbits went hopping by me along the inside of the guardrail. Maybe it's not as far back to nature from here as it seems.

We have silicon computer chips, people in space, global computer networks, mechanical hearts, turbo jet espresso machines, fax machines and microwave popcorn. An advanced culture that is a week's worth of groceries away from barbarism: When the hell, exactly, were poodles a wild animal?

I began thinking about the twenty-two cents or so left in my pocket and what the cost of a cab to Massachusetts, and subsequent family members, from here would be. I found thirty -five cents sitting in the middle of the first lane a few minutes later.

Yo, Taxi!

I didn't think it would make carfare, but at least I could call somebody who gave a shit.

I tried to remember what the area looked like on the map. Vaguely like pasta, I think.

I tried to figure out whether I had to pass through a corner of the city to get into the clear country of Connecticut, and whether I'd be able to get a ride there.

Concrete facts: this was I-95. It runs through my old hometown, and right past my high school. It also goes to Key West, where they watch the sunsets from the end of the pier as a community religion, but, the objective, the current effort, is North. I figured that I had two hundred miles to go to be near family: There is a shower and a bed there. So, if I got lucky, I'd be able to make Boston by morning.

Be it ever so humbling, there's no place like home.

The Jersey Turnpike Authority cruiser pulled in about then, moving like a square metallic shark in the darkness. I went through the regular routine of putting my bags down and carefully opening my jacket with my fingertips while they turned all the lights on me. I moved very slow; they had a lot of lights. A rack focus Christmas tree. I was even ready when they asked me what I was doing. Didn't even crack a grin.

It took some explaining, but not as much as it had in Michigan, to get them to understand that I was a college student, and not terribly dangerous in anything but an intellectual sense. And that only on my good days. I told them that my areas of study were History, Education and English.

From this they were able to surmise that I was going to school to be a School-Teacher. That wasn't far wrong, so I let them ask me about that for a while. Hell, I might end up being a Teacher.

They were both big paramilitary looking types, and within this paradigm, people come in two primary colors: Blue, and Not-Blue. One was older than the other.

They decided to give me a ride to get me off of the Turnpike, and because they seemed honestly worried about me.

New Jersey has always had a Police Reputation like the deep South, but I guess stereotypes aren't always true. After searching me, and my bags, and finding my (six inch, balanced, double edged) "cooking" knife, while still missing the hidden one, they gave me a ride.

I expected them to take that knife away from me and try to snap its blade against a curb. I say this because that is what cops usually do with other people's weapons, and I say "try to" because the blade is kind of unique. A sort of home made "Vegetarian Damascus": forged with nitrogen plant food, seawater and tofu for carbon, by a creatively demented friend on a mountain somewhere in the West.

One, professional, Cop-kick against a curb and I'd either be out a knife, or, more likely, have a hell of a lot of explaining to do as to why it wouldn't break. To a large, heavily armed, Trooper with a sore foot.

93

The Cop said, "You better keep it. You might need it". They locked it in the trunk for the duration of the ride though.

In the car I tried to ask them about the things that they'd seen out here. Cops get to see lots of really strange things and usually have good stories, and I am, after all, an English Major and Aspiring Writer Type. I've always loved talking with specialists in any field. Their ability to be totally immersed in their topic has always made me wish for a closeness like that. Few people get to be totally dedicated to a way of life anymore.

The response from them on the question "what's the weirdest thing you've seen out here?" was a resounding and immediate "You". Made me feel sort of, uh, special. They even did it in stereo.

They were listening to the police radio turned way down and a New York Rock station at a volume that I'd have turned down if a police car had pulled along side me. The station was playing a Pink Floyd "album side", and then one from Led Zeppelin. It was a little Clockwork Orange surreal for me: This was the music that I used to take drugs to.

I asked about it, and they wanted to know what I thought they'd be listening to.

"The Police radio", I said.

They both, in stereo again, said "boring" drawing out the "o" to limousine lengths. I didn't know how to respond to that, but it was funny.

I'm not sure exactly how long the ride was, but they were pretty friendly. Nice guys. Pointing out the Hudson River and various famous things on the way that they would probably show to any tourist. It was pretty cool. They took me right through the toll both into New York and dropped me off at Jerome Avenue in the Bronx next to a stripped out police car.

There seem to be a group of people in New York who will strip or graffiti anything that does not move. If it moves, they work faster. I once heard about a tourist from somewhere in the Midwest who got graffitied on the subway. I heard the story in North Dakota, as a warning to stay off the East Coast.

The older cop called me over to the car as I was putting my packs back on and asked me how much money I had on me, really. Made me show him my wallet and everything. I told him, and he gave me a dollar for coffee. I tried, as usual, to turn it down, but he insisted, and he was better armed and rested than myself.

I don't think that I can be even a little upset with those guys for dropping me off where they did. I'd more or less asked for it (though after one look I was willing to reconsider). It was the direction that I was headed in, and that buck, small as it might seem from the outside, was a pretty magnanimous gesture.

That buck still bugs me: The kindness of it. I didn't start the trip to be bumming money from people. I was just trying to get to school, so I could be smarter and a more productive member of Society. I didn't want to ask anybody for anything. I've been Homeless and have never panhandled. I still owe the world a lot of random kindness.

In some of the social contexts that I grew up in, I was taught that authority figures, especially Police, even the ones I am friends or relatives with were, potentially, the enemy.

The reality is a lot different.

Cops have a lousy job. Nobody ever calls them to a good time. Nobody likes to see them but their spouses and kids. They see people at their absolute worst, they have to, because even a "nice" person, when drunk or upset, can kill you. They might regret it like hell the next day, but that's a small consolation. That buck was a long reach from that world. Thanks, guys.

When they left I started walking again. I stopped to grab a lug nut lying next to the stripped cop car. Kind of a modern way of counting coup or the kind of souvenir that doesn't come from a gift shop.

The Cross Bronx Expressway is an old road cut through some of the granite and slate bedrock of the island. They made it wide enough for a sidewalk that nobody has probably used for walking in fifty years. It is of old, rounded, soft brick and is worn as smooth and shiny as water in some places. Every so often there are afterthought bridges that cut the walkway down to a few inches. Superseding design. It is covered in trash and there really wasn't anyplace to sit down.

I could hear some big rats rummaging in the trash piles near the rocks, and I didn't want to chance it. The people in New York have diseases that scare the hell out of me; I don't want to think about the rats.

After a while, I came to a place where the road is elevated, or rather, there is a broad valley smoothed with a bridge. The point is that I could not stick to the road.

Despite feeling claustrophobic, I was in no mood to enter this wider expanse; sometimes there is safety in small places.

I made it across the first major intersection before I was hailed by a woman dressed in tight jeans, a leather jacket and a baseball cap. She split off from a group of people who were talking and drinking wine around a fire in an oil drum under a bridge. She wanted to bum a cigarette, and I gave her one.

She asked me how much money I had, and what was I doing down here: I told her. She looked amazed. I guess she figured that I was uptown slumming, looking for drugs or some kind of sexual adventure. Maybe she thought I was a suicide looking to happen. It didn't start out that way, really.

In the city there are a thousand different kinds of tough guy. You can act or be as "Bad" as you want in the city; there will always be somebody tougher. Bad, Bad Leroy Brown and all that jazz. Many people in the city, any big city, take proving themselves to anyone who will pay attention as a full time job. Often it is all that there is to do. People do this act to the exclusion of survival or profit, maybe for the need to have something. Tough guys are an open target, but, nobody, nobody ever, fucks with a saint.

I wasn't out to do anything but pass through, similar to the battle scene in Little Big Man where they become invisible and just walk away. It's funny how you can just begin to need something that you've only just managed to be rid of.

Most real New Yorkers don't know there is anything in North America besides The City, Upstate, and maybe like Kansas or something. Nothing of interest between the Hudson and Hollywood.

I told her that if I had the money to, I'd buy her a cup of coffee and ask about how people live around here. I didn't have the money and she wasn't offering, so I left her standing there looking stunned.

I walked across the street, and then around a railroad track that a maintenance crew was working on.

Jack hammers and five hundred watt halogen work lights. Graffiti and rats. They had an armed guard.

They were not prisoners from jails, they were just trying to do their job, and they had an armed guard.

96

The large building on the other side of the tracks was the 84th precinct. I think that it's the one called "Fort Apache" in that Paul Newman movie. That was a little disconcerting. I kept walking and eventually managed to get back on the almighty highway a couple of miles later.

Going inland is probably a reasonable fear, at least for an American who grew up in an age where you can go to the bank, the movies or even out to dinner in a car. Most of the people I went to school with were probably conceived in cars, and altogether too many have and will die in them. What will happen when we run out of gas? Will a new form of anonymous, insulating, personal transport be developed? Or, Gods forbid, will we have to talk to each other and, like, walk?

Wars, racism, classism and discrimination stem from lack of interactive contact between people. Wars are hard to start without uniforms and isolation.

Mohammed Ali, the former world Heavy weight Boxing champion, who had once been named Cassius Clay, spent time in jail for refusing to go to war in Vietnam. His explanation was that no Commie ever called him a Nigger. He chose not to fight with anyone, outside of his professional context, including those who had denigrated him, and with special deference to those he did not know. There is a logic there that is so straightforward as to be nearly faultless.

In Boxing, Ali went against a single opponent, another man, in a test of physical strength and stamina, with equal opportunity for harm and the ability to use judgment.

In war people who are non-contestants die.

I have to admit that I've never liked Boxing. More of a Martial Arts guy, myself. It seems to me that two good athletes could find something more reasonable to do than beat the hell out of each other the way a tractor takes on a stump. But compared to War, it is a paragon of practicality.

When you are facing one adversary that you can measure yourself against, one human, then you can, at least, see what you are doing. Don't look at the uniform or the pigmentation, look at the person. If you are willing to take the time to see each individual as a separate entity, based on their assets and experiences, their strengths and contexts, then there is a possibility that you can learn something.

If everybody were willing to try to learn that lesson, group prejudice, hatred and fear would have less power than they do now.

In Denver, a couple of years ago, I was at a Martin Luther King Day rally. This was before all fifty states had accepted the holiday.

The Ku Klux Klan and some White Power assholes had been given a permit to hold their counter-demonstration on the steps of the capitol building.

Freedom of Speech allows them to advocate violence against other humans because of their melanin content and theological concepts. I'm all for that: free speech is good. Not always easy, but good.

Naturally, a riot broke out. Police cars were overturned. There was an old man there, in a striped paper uniform: he had survived Dachau. When the Klan attacked the protestors, he was screaming, "Go back to hell you bastards!"

About fifty of us had to protect him from them. The Klan was eventually herded aboard a city bus and taken away to a location where it was safer for them to be violent idiots. All this in the name of Dr. King, Jesus!

Several miles later, as I was crossing a huge flyover near an enormous white housing project, a big blue Mercedes 420 with New Jersey plates did a double U-turn to come back for me. I have seen very few people do anything as scary as that maneuver. Even in Boston driving.

The driver was a kind of yuppie looking guy in slightly too hip clothes.

In this context, a nylon jogging suit in pastel blue and yellow. He had a tan-a-rama/chemical moisturizer complexion, and hair styled to the point of looking freeze-dried. I've met a number of people who look sort of like this guy. Salesmen. Fashion slaves are weird, but not usually very dangerous. I'm on the right road. I'm out of the Bronx. Life is good. Any ride was welcome. How far to Boston?

He said that he was trying to find the way into the city so that he could be on Howard Stern's radio program.

You see, he had this theory about how being thin and in shape was a gift from Jesus and being overweight was the work of the Devil. He wanted to inform the world, so they could start rounding up all the fatties and raise their consciousness by lowering their weight. Your basic helpful guy. The Charlie Manson Diet Plan. Would I like one of these squeeze bottles of (really high in sugar) fruit punch? No, thanks, I'm trying to watch my weight.

The driver tried to articulate this complex theory to me, which sounded like a religious over-complication of Christian Fundamentalism and Pop-Psych Positive Body Image stuff. Kind of like what might happen if you cross Richard Simmons, on speed, with David Koresh, on a bad day.

He went on to detail how, if he could just get on "Howard's" show, he could save the world from eternal damnation by getting all those poor porky fat folks into fat farms and thusly save their souls. Beauty is good, ugly is evil. The Second Law of Thermodynamics must fall.

Have some Jim Jones fruit punch, it's on the diet plan. No, I don't want any fruit punch, thank you. Sure, I'll take some for later. Who knows how the day will go?

He told me of how many times he'd seen Stern, and where he parked his car and how great the guy is and what you have to do to get past security. Had all his books and tapes too.

Then he showed me his new invention, a spray bottle of water, like you would use for plants, that you could squirt in your face to wake yourself up. Neato. They should be available at the Buchenwald gift shop, alongside the juice and jackboot polish.

He sprayed himself a few times, directly in the face, and made this exaggerated shaking himself off motion. Like a primping drag queen or a poorly bred poodle having a seizure. I've always worn glasses; spray in the face makes it hard to see. Just as he asked me if I was tired, he sprayed me in the face twice with the silly thing.

I contemplated just casually killing him on the grounds that people this annoying should not be allowed out in sixty thousand dollar automobiles. If he started describing where we were by pointing to his hands, bad things were going to happen.

This freeze-dried fucking plastic android was a menace. I could see myself wrapping the seatbelt around his neck and the headrest until he stopped talking about his insane shit. I can't explain the reaction better than that; general revulsion: the sinister homo-erotic undercurrent of Nazi propaganda. To be the Master Race you have to be like them.

After we got through the tolls, I told him that this was my exit and that to get to lower downtown, he'd have to turn around and go back the way he came. Should have let him drive me to friggin' Boston. (Not that I want a thank-you note from Howard Stern.)

I gave him explicit directions back to the Lincoln Tunnel while getting my bags out of the car. He thanked me in that "just closed a deal, Sport-o" voice before he fully realized that he had to backtrack. He menaced me with his little teal-blue spray bottle again, without realizing that his Nike-clad foot had already stepped on the gas. He looked surprised that the car was moving.

A few minutes later, as he went roaring by in the other direction, I realized that my Boston sign was still in the back seat of his car. It was kind of a shame to lose it because I'd noted times, distances, mile markers and expenses on it. He made an obscene gesture at me out the window of the car, as it roared past in the other direction, clipped a jersey barrier in a splash of sparks, and accelerated though the tollbooth with an expensive German-car snarl.

Weird dude, I wonder what his keepers made of the sign?

So here I was again, on a road in the middle of somewhere at four thirty in the morning. Nothing to do but keep walking.

I remember calling my grandparents a while after I first got out to Colorado. I had been there for several weeks and I had just landed a job doing carpentry work.

As soon as my first paycheck came in I'd be able to live in something more substantial than my Chevy. My grandfather's advice was "keep working." Spartan and simple, little consolation at the time, but he had raised twelve children that way, so there had to be something to it. Thomas Hobbes ain't got nothing on my grandfather.

I kept walking. The road was wide, and the trees comfortingly close. It was a lovely red sunrise. The fact that the sun came up was a good omen, red or not.

I passed big suburban houses, horse paddocks and dew moist early morning gardens. Burgher America; sounds like a fast food chain.

Blow dryers and briefcases, Mommy's station wagon and Daddy's little red sports car waited dutifully in their places. There were early-morning lights on in modern kitchens and train stations.

I knew that there was a normal world around here somewhere.

Chapter 16

Leaving New York

"I was rappin' to the Fuzz, Man.
...the entire New York State Throughway is Closed, Man. Far out."
- Arlo Guthrie, At the 1969 Woodstock Music Festival

"We are all the same person trying to shake hands with ourselves."
- Wavy Gravy, At the 1969 Woodstock Music Festival

"The sixties generation grew up on dreams of love and peace. This flavor honors Wavy Gravy, the era's ultimate camp counselor who now says: 'The 90's are the sixties standing on your head.' The ideals of social justice and a healthy planet are the true legacies of the Woodstock Nation. It's up to all of us to bring them home and to have *fun* doing it. Enjoy signed Ben & Jerry."
- text on a package of "Wavy Gravy" flavor Ben & Jerry's Ice cream, August, 1994

Eventually, the breakdown lane ended and there were Jersey barriers with blacktop behind them. The road was cut out of higher, rock hardscrabble land. So, the blacktop backfill made a passable path about eighteen inches wide and about three feet above the roadbed. Not your ideal hitchhiking surface, but great for looking into convertibles. This was a fine way to walk, except for those places where the hill came up close on the right and the truck mirrors came by at shoulder and eye level.

Still, this worked out pretty well, until I got to the first overpass. No breakdown lane and a chain link fence on a steep hill to the right. Nothing to do but wait for a lull in traffic, jump out onto the road, run like hell to the other end of the bridge and climb back up. Did I mention that the traffic starts pouring out of the city towards New Rochelle and Connecticut around eight?

Busy ants swarm. Late pace in the day or something, delivery vehicles and sales critters fleeing the city core like roaches before the mighty Raid-empowered housewife. Lump-ety thump, lump-ety thump, circumventing bridges, circumnavigating a convenience. This routine got old pretty quick.

The body had been awake for too many days and just would not do it very fast. The big muscles in the thighs had turned rubbery and sludgy. Good maintenance is a sign of elegance. Rich folks get to wear thin shoes. Unmaintained tools fail. By the seventh or tenth bridge I'd had about enough.

I sat down for a while, before what I hoped was the last overpass, took off my mandatory denim jacket, brushed my teeth (after you've been awake that long and smoked that many cigarettes, they get to feeling like a baby komodo dragon has been using your mouth for a potty chair) with water from my canteen. Colorado water. Is this possible? Where is home? What is home?

I ate the very last handful of my lovingly packed Colorado granola, savoring cashews and chocolate chips, and buried the paper bag under a rock, just like they showed us in Boy Scouts.

I sat in the American version of lotus and indulged the luxury of things that should be breakfast. Daydream outdoor breakfast, on a late summer morning on the porch of an old house in the woods. In slanting golden sunlight.

Meditational groove: Om Mani Padma Muffins. An omelet would be good, with sharp cheddar, mushrooms and french roast coffee. Maybe blueberry muffins, and sparkling grape juice with Kenyan Double A. Key lime pie, the New York Times and Jamaican Blue Mountain (with heavy cream and brown sugar). Strawberry crepes with pineapple juice and Italian Roast. Can the Inquisition bust you for the decadence of chocolate Raspberry coffee? Starbucks smooth Kona? Would a Spanish Dark Roast be acceptable?

Wait, who the hell invited the Inquisition to Breakfast? A call goes up from their table in the voices of Monty Python, "Nobody expects the Inquisition!". Luther, the old waiter grumbles "Non Servium" under his breath.

I think I prefer to eat alone, perhaps with a little light music: Bach's Goldberg Variations, Fleetwood Mac's Rumors album, some long and winding instrumentals from The Allman Brothers. Old music: "A blast from the past" says an AM Radio DJ voice in my head.

A sure enough, biologic function. After stuffing myself on a couple of imaginary breakfasts, that old after breakfast urge hits. At least the neighbors didn't call about the volume of the music. Good digestion can be a real drag at times. Time to find a restroom.

I put my jacket back on and looked at the high chain link fence. Government project, and just for show. Technically speaking, it was a fence, just not a really good one.

They asked one of the astronauts what he was thinking, sitting on top of the biggest skyrocket ever constructed, and he said that it was made out of however many millions of parts, all made by the lowest bidder. Fortunately, so was this fence.

The twist wires that held the mesh to the uprights were not much stronger than, say, bread bag closures. I undid a few of them and wriggled under the fence.

Then I wriggled back and got the roll of toilet paper out of my pack and wriggled back again.

I found a nice secluded spot that was, albeit, thirty feet from the highway and maybe thirty feet from the road over it, fairly secure. Amidst some kind of broadleaf plant, over some poison ivy, and shaded by a couple of beech trees I did what I had to do there, and tried not to get too low. Poison Ivy is not fun.

As I was wriggling back under the fence, I heard a couple of voices. Two joggers were passing within five feet of where I had just been! I tore a huge piece out of the shoulder of my trusty old denim jacket getting under that fence quick. I packed up and went around another bridge. Fast.

I saw my first New York State Trooper around nine o'clock. I was sitting down just short of some roadwork on the other side of the highway. Staring, in Georges Seurat soft focus blank, at some tall grass, cat o'nine tails going to seed, near a brook and thinking about girls in Victorian sundresses and big hats. A lacy parasol protecting the fair skin of a young girl in a boat. Picnic in the park without the consciousness of Seurat's pixilated dots. Not that much focus.

The day and the place had that hazy fantasy quality of some of the late impressionists. Hudson River School, Huh? I thought they were making it up. Indefinable bits of pollen fluff in the diaphanous air, and the distinct edges of things gone into soft focus for the first time in days. You could almost hear a tinny Victrola in a rowboat and taste the sweet lemonade in tall sweating glasses.

He pulled in behind me and, I guess when I didn't turn around, he felt it necessary to blare his siren at me. I bet all of those dirty grubby little artist types were as annoying to the Victorians.

I was about twenty feet in from the road and celebrating the fact that the Jersey barrier and bridge nonsense had finally come to an end. There was a road widening project going on over on the other side of the road from my Victorian fantasy, maybe I was spacing out pretty badly.

But, the nice officer brought me into his reality very quickly. He got on the bull horn, after he had my attention, and said "You aren't hitching, are you Son?"

I shook my head vigorously no. I'd been meditating in some fashion. And I'm not your son. So that would be a, like double negative, right?

He said that was good and that I should enjoy my nature walk and be careful not to turn on any two-way radios because of the blasting. I nodded and thought, somewhat irrationally perhaps, that I've known a number of two way radios; I was never their type. Get out of my fantasy Officer. Radio doesn't exist yet. Neither do you.

I know that I was looking at that creek for over an hour, maybe three. Because the first dynamite blast was at ten. Scared the hell out of me.

I thought the only thing worse than rumpled impressionist painters with dirty fingers and atrocious table manners showing up at Victorian picnics was, perhaps, ants. Or was that Aunts? Who sent for this guy dressed like a paramilitary Blueboy? I got up and started walking again.

I was having no luck whatsoever with my sign, and my body was beginning to give up on me. The leg muscles had turned liquid. I felt betrayed, and I wished I'd been born with a different sign, but at least I had some warning.

Around noon I was stopped by another member of the fine, fraternal brotherhood of New York State Police. We did the same dance that I've described before.

Maybe some dance school could benefit from this stuff. Put down backpack, one, two, other bag, one, two, open jacket (in this case, loose shirt over tee shirt, as it was about ninety degrees and humid, and you have to be ready to improvise at all times) three, four.

104

I know a number of police officers; I have attended potluck dinners and religious gatherings with them, played chess with a couple, and discussed philosophy and politics with others. I know that they are not stupid people. The profession precludes survivability with a substandard intellect. Why the hell do these guys have to ask me what I'm doing?

It would seem pretty evident, wouldn't it? You'd think the sign would be a dead give away. I've met people from Tibet and New Zealand who know about hitchhiking. My Grandparents and their Parents before them had, at least, heard of it.

This particular officer looked as though he had never seen a pedestrian before and asked to see every bit of identification I had. (He probably would have felt better if I had a V.I.N. number tattooed somewhere and a proof of insurance card.) He let me go after checking me for wants, warrants and working taillights.

I sat down for a bit, after that one left, and contemplated just going to sleep. Nice water, pretty grass, dynamite alarm system across the road. I guess I should have, but I kept having visions of being a frozen fur trapper pinning a note to my chest to explain how I came to be here.

I kept walking. It seemed like less effort than putting all the words down on paper.

Around quarter to three, (did you ever notice that since digital clocks, quarter to three is now 2:45, or 2.45.32 E.S.T.?) with no break in sight, and no place for people to stop for me, I met the same police officer. I said "hi".

He was standing next to his car in the breakdown lane on the other side of the highway. When I got up even with him he yelled "Hey you" at me. This guy had seen every bit of identification that I carry, he knew my mother's maiden name and where I had been manufactured, and he could damn well address me by name. I ignored him.

He got on his bullhorn and tried again. Boy, it was a nice one and I guess he liked it a lot. He sounded kind of upset so I stopped and looked over at him. He was red in the face, and I hoped it was o.k. for him to be yelling like that.

He asked me if I knew that hitchhiking was against the law on this road. He must have found a dictionary somewhere.

I shook my head: no.

He told me that the exit in front of me was mine. I wanted to thank him politely and refuse out of courtesy but could not find a way to explain, across eight lanes of moving highway traffic, how difficult it would be to transport the ungainly bastard of concrete and asphalt home.

Can I carry an Einstein backpack that lets you fold one of these things to the size of a matchbook? An infinite bag of holding, with access to other dimensions? N-space? What if it falls out of my pocket somewhere in Nebraska? What if I forget and run it through the laundry?

He sensed my confusion and told me that I couldn't walk on this, his, road anymore.

I nodded agreement across the eight lanes. I didn't feel like walking on it anymore either. What kind of conversation is this? Is he enjoying this particular transactional level of discourse? Do you get along with your family well if you enjoy this flow direction?

He went on to explain to me through his chromed bullhorn that if he did not see me go up that ramp that he would arrest me. He looked like he wanted to come across all eight lanes and strangle me for not telling him in the first place that what I was doing was hitchhiking and it was against the law.

He'd just thought I was out for a rather odd walk perhaps?

Well, that would be true.

The Aussies have a thing called "walkabout", which is a sort of Zen-like exploration of interior and exterior landscapes. If I ever have time I may take one.

Brilliant people, those "Aborigines". Western man has lost the light nature of questioning within spirituality. Religion, they call it. Centuries ago we in the West used to do it. The American Indians do Vision Quests, but they take it very seriously, then again, I suppose they have to. It's about all they have left.

Our "Holy Books" supposedly know all the answers and we do not feel the need to go see things for ourselves. Been a problem since The Crusades. Attitude problem. Just check the list.

Jesus, the carpenter of Nazareth was a blonde white guy with blue eyes and a sparse beard? Not very fucking likely.

Fundamental flaw in the system of Deity removed one step from the individual: simple people are afraid to see all that was made by that which created the whole thing. That's why they take a book that has over a dozen points of view on some events literally. Timid.

If you dare to take all the time that you need to go see something that interests you, sort of like the way Steinbeck defines "Vassilado" in Travels With Charlie, you can learn personal truths about how it all fits together. Things that matter in a way that only makes sense to you. Spirituality is deeply personal and kind of time consuming. You will probably be late for the office.

Compared to the calm, contemplative nature of that spirit of exploration, that boldly thrown muse, I was having a spastic existential fit. Steinbeck said, "We don't take a trip, a trip takes us". I felt like a traitor to the road, allowing suburban Officer Friendly to scare me.

The Walkabout is as sacred to the Aborigines in Australia as the Vision Quest is to the Indigenous people of North America. We, in our infinite genius to do things the easy way, we have cable television. It's sort of the same, if you squint.

Walkabout is even legal, to the best knowledge of myself and the friendly officer, but the explanation would sound a little strange. Gee, isn't public educational television a wonderful thing?

Having figured out that I was actually hitchhiking, he was getting pretty red in the face, and I didn't want him to get in existential trouble. I still maintain that the sign was a dead give away. "Playland", it said.

I took the exit. It didn't fit in my pocket so I left it where it was, pockets being one of the Creators mistakes, but it's still mine. Please remember. The sign said Rye, Harrison, Playland.

If I'd have had any spirit of fun left in me I'd have gone to Playland just to see what it was like. I imagined a whole community resembling the kid-land at fast food restaurants. I might have been too scary looking to let in though.

A friend of mine says that when she was a kid she thought that clowns were a separate species: and really scary. I tried not to imagine brightly painted fiberglass houses that looked like tall shoes. Foundations of half buried automobile springs, doors like the mouths of giant clowns, a little dementia under the smog-berry trees. It had to look like that, but it was okay, I'd check it out later.

In New York, no matter how normal it looks, somebody weirder than you has already been there. I still can go look around up there anytime I want: I own the only exit ramp.

I'd been walking alongside some train tracks from time to time and it didn't occur to me to see what the fare was. I probably could have made the same distance that had taken me all day for about a dollar, and I had one. It was getting grim out and I needed to stop soon.

Harrison was pretty solid sounding. Lets see.

Chapter 17

Harrison

"Beyond the reach of human range, a drop of hell, a touch of strange"
— Roland Deschain, from The Gunslinger by Stephen King

"People are strange when you're a stranger, faces look ugly when
you're alone..."
- People Are Strange, Jim Morrison

I walked into Harrison, found a small department store and bought a little bottle of orange juice with most of my precious buck, and swiped a dozen little packets of salt from the snack bar. Dehydration prevention.

Gotta keep the old electrolytes up. Live in a desert and you learn these things so well that they run on autopilot. It helps. I was.

A Medic friend of mine carries, at summer events where people are likely to pass out from dehydration and overexertion, a gallon of stuff called "Bat Sweat". Potassium salts and Gatorade. If it tastes good, you are in seriously bad shape. When it tastes bad, stop. By the time you get re-hydrated you can think that clearly.

The hinterlands, though scenic, can be a Bitch.

Little cartoon voice in my head says: "Look Yogi, a telephone."

I called my grandparents and told my grandfather the situation was as best I could. He told me that he didn't know what to do, and that my grandmother, who usually handles the emergency situations in the family, would be back in an hour and a half. Could I call back?

Gee, sure. Never heard him flustered before. Hmmmm. Violation of the protocol: communication usually goes through my grandmother.

I hung out around town for a bit, trying to look casual, while seeking a public bathroom, and not being too out of place among the people in full Brooks Brothers costume who commute daily into New York.

Failing that, I decided to make a couple of collect calls to let some people know I was only a short distance away. It was four in the afternoon and, with luck, I'd be home the next day. Human not long after that.

I have in my possession a phone book of sorts. Scuffed brown leather with brass corners and often leafed through pages that are alphabetized by a system of associations only I seem to find sensible. If properly understood, it shows more about my life, my true self, than I've ever directly told anyone.

The last known numbers for friends and or their families. People, living and dead, that I haven't seen for ten years or more are next to truck repair shops, ethnic bakeries, radio stations and dive bars that may not even still exist. There are listings for Universities and motorcycle repair shops in all parts of the country, neatly listed near computer software people in the East Bay, Seattle, Denver and Boston, Inter-library loan offices right next to the phone number for Cafe Du Monde in New Orleans.

If looked at without explanation these things are probably more disjunctively alien than an unguided photo album, or the contents of someone else's attic, each has their own memories, stories, tales and intimate connections.

The friends would probably be surprised at each other, Computer Programmers, herbalists and Cops. A woman who plays the harp. Witches, Buddhists, Catholics and Radical Lesbian Feminists. A practicing Atheist who is an ordained Minister. A Methodist Minister who would be happier if he could be an Atheist. Ex-girl-friend's, Bookstores in odd cities, Odd bookstores in regular cities, cheap restaurants and the midnight phone numbers of a few underground Newspaper and 'Zine editors.

There are coffee shops where they do poetry slams and readings, folk music and hardcore punk, computer bulletin boards with family topic areas and pirate data, train stations' phone booths, and an organic health food Bakery in Brattleboro, Vermont that I've always been kind of partial to. Their slogan is "To work less efficiently, we need more people!"

I think the meanings and connections of these people, places and events show me, from time to time, the places I've been and the things I've known and done more clearly than anything else. Their names live in my little phone book. Sometimes, late at night, I take it out and wonder what is happening, in the places and to the people that I care about, whether they are loved or lonely, whether or not

110

they laughed today. Sometimes I find that a whole page has numbers for dead people or those who've moved with no forwarding. Sometimes I even take those pages out.

My father was not home when I called, and neither were most of the friends I tried. That happens too.

I called Janet's house. I used to live next door to them when we were in high school. I knew Jan first, so I always think of it as her house. Janet, her sister Sheryl, brother Michael, and I had gotten in our share of trouble together as teenagers and they, of all the people I knew, are probably more like family than my own. Friends. (Their father, who has a degree in nuclear physics, is known as Dangerous Dave the Electrician: He can do amazing things to radios.)

Together we have probably drunk a thousand gallons of barely palatable coffee, and spent a year or two of cumulative time in late night restaurants trying to figure out how life worked. They, probably more than my own family, see me pretty clearly, and we don't have anything much invested in putting each other on. They even seem, though it might be delusion on my part, to speak, through inevitable, these days largely symbolic, sibling rivalry, to each other a little better when I'm around.

Ring-Ring!

Collect from Joe?!!!

Gumbo ya-ya, familial crosstalk, multi-layered conversation. I never expected Sheryl to say, in her highest and most excited voice, in the middle of our four person conference call, "Where are you!?; We'll come get you!" less than thirty seconds into the call. Hell, it had only been a couple of years since we had last seen one another.

Home is the place, as Hemingway said, where, when you go there, they have to take you in. Yea, but do you deliver? I gave them rough directions and they said they'd see me as soon as they could.

There was a clean, well-lighted place to go to now. I'd live. Cool. That was the highest objective. If I'm going to die, I want a bath and some dinner first. Maybe a little music.

In that minute the rubber band snapped. The direction of pull, tying me to my tenuous home in the West, changed. I went from being two thousand miles from home, alone, dirty, and totally exhausted, to being, I don't know, precious? Loved? Valued? I knew that I had a chance to make it.

I hung out there, in the middle of suburban Harrison, trying to look like I belonged. I had once, in a suburban town, a bit north of Boston. It looked a lot like this one. Straight suburbia. Station wagons, crab grass, and good schools. A scary alien world now, with the subtle and creeping undertones of Stepford families with perfect teeth and organized lives. Daytimers, Bar-Bee-Que grills, network television and Family Values.

I wondered about the private lives and secret thoughts of these shiny, happy people. It looked too much like a trip to the shopping mall.

Did they have hardcore bondage gear, carried home in their shiny new station wagons and mini-vans, fetish toys lurking on their closet shelves? Did they secretly want to run amok with lawnmowers, designer kitchen appliances or machine guns? How many of them see analysts or have a little problem with scotch or prescription drugs? What did they really think? Could life be this clean and ordinary? What do they do here?

I kept expecting sitcom characters to walk by me in rare, off set, location shots. I pulled out a notebook and did a couple of bad sketches of the train station and its catwalk. The signs and Broadway show posters looked, then and now, scary and threatening or too bright and garish. The poster for the show "Cats" looked feral.

I never could draw worth a damn. The parking meters all look like metallic flowers from Mars and, on every corner there are obscene little blue boxes that squat and digest mail.

I sat in the train station, with a notebook in my lap, balanced on an unlimber knee, the leather bound, brass cornered, phone book showing out of the corner of my pack. I tried to look like one of them, doing some really weird act.

They say New Yorkers can wish anything invisible, and Kitty Genovese's ghost could testify to that. After Michigan I knew about invisibility. Pull it around like a shroud. Cloaking device activated, Captain. I didn't want anybody to really see me now, and the tenuous magic, stretched thin over many miles, held.

I guess it worked. If I were any weirder looking, it would not have worked as well. Nike's and Levi's and Banana Republic shirts were enough to pass, as long as I stayed downwind.

Too funky for here. If anybody had asked, I'd have played the renegade sculptor or counter culture writer: what the hell, I've been both at different times.

The affected grunge of the "ratty preppie" look from my early teens started in New England Prep Schools long before my time, and the New York Suburbanites have taken it in as their own. Rub the gloss off the gold card for it. Maybe I was somebody else's kid, pretending to be just in from Colorado or Montana or someplace.

You can't get grunge like this in the 'burbs, but they didn't know that. I practiced speaking in rounded couplets in my head, so I could deal with the mundanes in the expected manner, and the ghost of Shakespeare went out for a drink to keep from doing backflips in his grave. Ogden Nash and Walt Whitman got a case of beer and went out for a ride. Aristotle went out to work in the garden. Plato laughed and pointed to Dante's door. Pirsig's altered ego cocked one of his lupine eyebrows, looked me in the eye and said "Quality act Man, but they know better."

After all that motion, it was surprisingly hard to keep still. A goddamned fool off the hill. The rhythm of the road, tires on the highway and footfalls on pavement had become what awake meant. Thumpety thump thump, thumpety thump. Motion as mantra. The road as moving mandala. Thumpety thump. License plate glyphs and toll booth temples. Sticky-Notes from the Gods on the side of the highway in Iowa. Thumety thump, grass in the bumper, thump.

I walked from one side of the platform to the other. Sit meditatively on one bench, get up and stretch, move to another, repeat as needed. Motion as Mantra.

There was an enclosed catwalk, like a low budget New England covered bridge, corrugated steel faded sea-foam green and brown wood, over the tracks.

When the fog came flowing in at about eight o'clock, and the shiny silver express trains tossed teal and ultramarine sparks against the black the air tasted like a new penny. The overhead catenary supports were hard gleaming brass and copper; the sparks were three yards of smooth moving lightning. Seeing everything with Nikola Tesla's eyes. Did Ming the Merciless design this thing?

It seemed like a transportation mode that should be indigenous to the planet Mongo, somehow akin to the gas stations of the thirties and forties with their laser ray gun emplacements and flying wings. Hugo Gernsback's Art Deco turrets poised to defend the Bijou.

Things had the painful acuity of vision that Artists, Real Artists, not fools like me, try to convey in their best work. Van Gogh's Starry Night, Munch's Scream. Hemingway not eating for a day or two so he could appreciate the mastery of Cézanne. Poe's protracted nightmares and the high, brittle, maniacal edge to Mozart's brilliance, Bach's fugues.

Eyes wide and super-fried. I suffered for my art and now it's your turn sucker. The brightest light burns half as long. The edge is brilliant but very, very sharp. Carbon arc lightning, works every time.

The best artist's work sells high after their death because they die too quickly. The art exists elsewhere and uses them as a conduit. They know how to work and shape and bend their form, and everybody else spends decades learning to understand or imitate it.

It's a kind of fire, an all consuming fire that burns in the blood. You have to wait until they die, and they always do, because art can kill you, for the work to sell. Because, real artists, justifiably, will wring the life out of you if you say "Hey, Buddy, how much you want for that thing?" Art is anything you can get away with. Art can kill. Don't piss them off. So uncouth...

It is said that the reason people need sleep is to have time to process and sort subconscious thoughts. Time for the impressions of the day to percolate through the gravel of the conscious and suspend themselves in the mind's aquifer. I read somewhere that you could just lay down for half an hour a day if your subconscious were clean. But we all need filters - too much energy, and information coming at you all the time. Like that alleged symphony where the guy walks on to the stage and turns on twenty-nine radios and spins the dial. Life is like a radio dial, or something. There is too much input for existing physiological modes, and the strain is showing.

Maybe with sub-processing in the background, and a full multiplexed connection between the (at least) two sides of the personality, you can go forever, theoretically. Sleep is a battle, for some, to filter the dirty little secrets of the day.

A Buddhist monk I met somewhere said that you can go without sleep for the rest of your physical life if you want to, but you'd be talking about a matter of months. He used to be a big acid eater, but he said he gave it up because he'd rather take the stairs than the elevator. He said killing yourself was wasteful because he couldn't see why you would not bother to get your soul dry cleaned while you're here. Pushing the edges of perception was a good and useful hobby, but you would probably enjoy inner peace more. He also gave me a flower, and got mad when I wouldn't chant with him.

Around Midnight, I was standing there on the platform, with darkness full upon it. I was at a medieval banquet in some old and disused building. Maybe in the city somewhere. A place I knew would appear abandoned to anyone else. Just left of reality. Many of my friends were there, in costumes from various periods. The men in chainmail or kilts or classic cutaway tailcoats, the ladies resplendent in their Elizabethan, Victorian and Second Empire gowns.

They were bedecked in jewels and their best finery. Silken and linen peacocks. A hundred shades of blue and green, scarlet and gold. Snoods woven with emeralds and yards of silk and lace. Gem encrusted sword hilts and silver drinking cups flashed from a hundred places at once. Rich tallow-candle golden light. Musicians that I could not see played the Mozart duets for violin and harpsichord. Silver and jewels on every hand. Intricately carved wooden plates and bowls laden with green grapes and oranges on silk embroidered linen tablecloths. White and green candles, for it was Beltane, gleamed in brass and silver sticks among the golden and red flowers.

I remember the flavor of the mutton and mead. Hell, I could taste it, and it was more real than many meals I've had to pay for. The fulfillment of warm food and perfectly balanced drink filled me in some way that I'd always sought without being able to define. Like the warm glow of love or the deep satisfaction of certainty. They say to never eat in dreams, or you'll have to stay.

I was drinking rich honey mead from a large goblet made of fine wrought silver wire, green glass and blue gem stones. The best Celtic artisan of two thousand years ago would have spent years of his life making it. The jeweled inlays and bas relief of Cernunnos and Bridget on the chalice were as real as this book in your hands. The gods were alive, and the feast was rich.

I only realized that it was an illusion when I reached to put the goblet down on a long, heavy, oaken table and the table was not there.

As I recovered my balance, the goblet and the rest of the beautiful scene were gone. I held on tight, but they tumbled back behind their veil. There was nobody else on the platform. The torches

115

in their wall sconces had vanished in a twinkling wink, along with the innumerable members of the feast. I hope that I did not speak aloud; I'd just made a very bawdy toast to the beauty and wellbeing of the ladies.

I sat down, trying to recapture that perfect place, like some traveler of old, missing Brigadoon. The loss of that beautiful place was one of the most tangible of my life and it feels, even today, like a phantom missing limb. If that is heaven, Valhalla, or The Great Whatever, I want to go back someday.

Some unspecified time later Sheryl was standing in front of me. I did not greet her until I had carefully touched her hand to make sure that she was real. When she was, I hugged her a little too hard and a little too long. The words of family greeting spoken, in some way understood. The innate knowing of kin and safety.

They tell me I push too hard on my cross-country sprints. I have been found, a day or more ahead of schedule, in dusty disreputable battle-scarred cars, parked in the driveways of the expectant friends and family, with a note on my windshield reading: "Hi, my name is _____. Give me a cookie and a bath and send me to bed and I'll tell you how I got here tomorrow".

It is sometimes said that I have a bit much of a flair for the dramatic. Some people just think I'm a fool.

At least, so far, I've always gotten the right house. And everybody says they forgive me.

Chapter 18

Catching Up

"No matter how dreary and gray our homes are, we people of flesh and blood would rather live there than in any other country, be it ever so beautiful. There is no place like home."
- Dorothy, from The Wizard of Oz by Frank Baum

It took them most of the night to drive down and get me, and all the rest of it to drive back. Janet bundled up her two-year-old son, who I had never seen before, and Sheryl bundled both of them into the minivan.

They drove all night, I 84 & I 95, in seamless tag team conversation, the way the Sisters usually talked. I don't know if I was awake or not.

I knew I was going home in some way, and that everything would be all right. Adventures are nice, but as Mr. Baggins pointed out, it is good to go home. I probably did sleep, neglecting my sacred duty to tell the tale of the road.

In the old days, at least in the British Isles, even a fleeing Criminal would stop to pass on news. It's a scared trust.

Janet just barely got back in time to get to work at six. Her husband, as usual, was pretty jealous: I seem to have that effect on him. This usually has positive benefits for Jan, who, having gone civilized in her late twenties, doesn't mind the extra attention.

I took a shower, with family members ducking through the bathroom to say hi as they went off to work. Afterwards, which is to say several hundred gallons of hot shower later, I tried to tell the story to Sheryl, as far as you've now read it, over a mountainous breakfast, but it wouldn't come out right, so there had to be more to come.

She, by means of some family telegraph that I just about halfway understand, would fill everybody else in. She even asked the questions that different family members would be interested in, so that I'd only have to tell the story once and fill in details of the shape for others later.

I was not entirely successful in relating the events that caused me to be checking her physical reality on a commuter platform in Harrison, New York, at nearly One in the morning, but she listened and patiently let me try.

Their house is a glorious tumble of life lived fully and well. An early nineteenth century sort of farmhouse that had been, at least for a while, earlier in the century, a funeral home. It is royal blue with white trim, and nearly in town.

The town grows, the house stays put. A happy match and mismatch of the changing styles of a century and a half of tolerable family taste, eclectic interests and sporadic antique and rummage sale acquisition. Hall-trees and Ham Radios. Italian crystal glasses and a juice box left on an old school-desk.

The corners are cluttered with working or half-working interesting gadgets; spread over four parlors and probably twice as many bedrooms. You don't use the phrase "what is this doing here?" without specifying. These walls had boomed with laughter and jokes and crying shouts of the unbearable pain of life for a long time and the house felt a contented fulfillment for it. Old houses need to be lived in.

The kitchen floor was painted particle board, as it had been back in high school, because the hardwood had been destroyed or removed for restoration as a result of some story that I had never heard all of.

The dining room table was still the same enormous glossy pine plateau that served the house variously as geographic, message and psychic center, resplendent with keys and kids toys and a current newspaper. The curved glass-front china cabinets still held the prized china and glassware of five generations of women. The hundred-year-old imitation Gainsborough landscape still hung above the sofa. There was still a partially rebuilt oscilloscope under some winter hats next to the hall tree near the stairs.

The house was still half rebuilt, and probably always would be. It must be something to do with the entropic nature of big old houses that lots of people actually live in. It'd never make a center spread in Bigger Homes and Garages, but who cares?

For one reason or another "the kids", now in their mid to late twenties, were all living back at home with their parents. Jan's husband had recently gotten out of the Navy, and they were both working to support themselves and two kids in the inevitable collapse

118

after the end of the Reagan/Bush years. Michael, the brother, was working a good job and saving for a house and Sheryl had just gone back to school to finish her degree. Everybody took a turn with Jan's two kids.

We talked for four hours and as many pots of dark black coffee. We compared notes on life.

Who had gotten married, had children or moved away. What they got for their house, and what kind of hell the town was going to because of all the new folks moving in. Who had died and how and how we felt about it. Who was dying and what we could do.

The intervening time, for a brief few hours, sloughed off, and I felt almost as though I had never left home. My accent came back. I remembered which drawer the coffee spoons lived in and got assigned babysitting duty for three hours on next Thursday afternoon.

The streets had been moved a bit, and some of the back roads had been, unimaginably, paved and some swampy house lots sold to fools from somewhere else, but all was essentially the same.

Small towns rarely ever really change. A few new friends, a few more of the old ones dead for different reasons ranging from stupidity, booze and car accidents (a decreasing category now that thirty is in sight for the peer group) to A.I.D.S (sadly, a growing category) and still the occasional suicide.

After a full morning of checking the connections and telling the tales, Sheryl got her key ring, the one that could double as a snow chain for a small farm tractor, down from the peg by the kitchen phone, and we went to look at the changes since I'd been gone. Another leg on the trip; over the river, and though the woods to Grandmother's house...

Much had changed, and the rain, which had mercifully stayed out of my way for the whole trip, began now with a rifle sharp crack of lightning. The rain ran down the windows, and I watched the little droplet worms slide up and back as the car rolled through a place I used to call home.

Chapter 19

A Sort of Homecoming

"Seasons don't fear the reaper...."
-Blue Oyster Cult

It was raining in late May and I was home.

Sheryl drove her old red Buick land yacht through the heart of the old town. I looked out the window at the mingled rain and hail. I felt like a ghost. Three hundred and fifty years old and full of the memories of my ancestors and the ghosts of history. My family had always lived near here.

Every little jerk-water town in Massachusetts has memories of some kind and selling postcards and souvenirs of the more picturesque ones to the Tourists is a legitimate industry. The place is so fucking picturesque that there are always a few fender benders each fall involving Tourists gawking at the leaves and asking if it's the peak of the foliage yet.

There's a Carnegie library in the best Gothic style of 1892 and a shiny new Exxon station. The Towne Butcher Shoppe and the twenty-four hour convenience store crouch at opposite ends of the Square like mortal enemies. Or more like "before and after" pictures.

Further on, at the unfashionable end of town, near a crumbling Art Deco gas station, there was an old train station turned corner store, and Jack's Donut Shoppe.

And there was the cemetery where we had buried Jesus and The Kid my senior year in High School.

The Kid had been one of the good ones, probably born old, with a wisdom and a peace in his eyes that even dying slow couldn't dim. He was a thirteen-year old.

Champion motocross rider and all-state soccer player and he'd gone out tough.

Leukemia.

His family was what they would call "working poor" or something nowadays, but who the hell wasn't. Five kids, no father, his Mom drove a school bus for a living.

I'd never heard him say a bad word about anybody, and everybody who had ever talked to him had been impressed. People wouldn't even smoke dope around him because he didn't like the smell and couldn't abide talking to the stoned. He was like that even before he got sick. He was okay.

Jesus was a punk and nobody was going to miss him anyway. His father had given him the nickname, and not much else, because of the length of his hair. I doubt many people associate his real name with him anymore.

I'd been pretty tight friends with both of his kid brothers, and kind of knew him from around town. I still have the six hash-mark Zippo lighter he gave me when, at fifteen, I started smoking and he was trying to quit. He had taught me how to make strawberry crepes when I was about ten. At thirteen he showed me those long solos on Allman Brothers and Santana albums, even got me hip to Bach and Mozart. Back when he still cared about things.

The last time I saw him he was living in a rented room over a bar in Salem and working in a pool hall or something.

The Kid had gone down honest and rock steady, a death with honor that shamed you to see. The world doesn't make many people with that kind of full peace very often. What almost nobody knew was that Jesus had been almost as good, but not quite as lucky.

Jesus had a couple of jailhouse tattoos, a simple cross and an oddly angular grim reaper, done in shoe polish with a thread wrapped sewing needle. Said the first was a joke on his name, and the second his reality. He said they both represented God.

He was maybe twenty at the time, and that seemed old enough to have picked a path in life. I know he believed that nothing could really get to him, and he bought the farm in a stolen red three hundred horsepower '68 Pontiac Tempest, and I think he could have done better.

He went out fast, without really believing life could be about anything else.

He blew it on a slick back road trying to make that twisty little jump and curve out by the old abandoned factory on School Street. Death by attempted ascension or something.

121

Split the car in half at the dashboard and the funeral was a low buck closed casket affair.

I don't really remember what the weather was like that Spring. Ordinarily, I wait so long for Winter to be over that I mark the weeks, indelible for their counting each year, in my mind.

I know it rained hard, turning into hail the night Jesus died. The weather had been gray rain and pure white hail like it was this, the day of my homecoming, and the day we buried him.

The late spring ground of the cemetery was frozen in a hard crystal frost that crunched and crackled like wine glasses under our boots.

Everything was chrome gray frost over deep green and brown: brittle and acutely sharp.

There wasn't anybody there over twenty but Old Sam, the drunk from the low budget church across town.

I think Jesus was Catholic, but we never really talked about it.

I read, in The Golden Bough, I think, that some of the old Gods would hide the small stone that was their soul so nobody could ever find it.

Maybe that's just how the game is played.

Tight jeans with rips aren't really that comfortable, and the carefully casual unlaced steel-toe boots get your feet wet in the rain. Concert t-shirts under leather or denim don't really protect from the elements. You have to be tough. But, it's a long reach to show human values from behind those masks.

There were maybe thirty people standing in the old bone yard for Jesus, trying to express ourselves somehow, in grief, shivering out of respect. Doing it our way, more out of necessity than style.

The best gesture of defiance and class we could do. Black leather jackets and nickel chrome studs shined with shoe and metal polish to show respect for the dead. When you are tough, you have to look it, and it takes time to affect the perfect look.

Jeans and boots and black leather.

Some of us dressed that way because it was all we had.

Different people, of the hundred or so to later say they were there, said that they'd have played some appropriate piece of loud rock music to show some class, but couldn't find the tape or the stereo had broken or something.

There was no appropriate piece of music. Nobody knew what the fuck to say.

We didn't die man, we were teenagers, and Jesus was the first guy to be bad enough to be tossed out of school, to have been disowned by his folks. He disowned them right back.

He was pretty tough, but he went out stupid. At least he went out fast.

The Kid had not had it so lucky. It had taken months for the chemotherapy to make him too weak to stand, and almost nobody knew him towards the end.

He was still in there though, still behind his own eyes. His cousin took him to school, in a wheelchair, for an hour, about a week before he died. I heard him laugh with somebody.

His funeral procession had everybody from school there.

The Vice Principal announced that anybody caught attending would be on detention for two weeks. We policed ourselves. Anybody who cut classes that day and not attended had, according to the custom of their clique, gotten some form of physical or social retribution.

I heard, a couple of years later, from a Cop who was there, that the line of cars was something over four miles long.

Detention hall was filled to bursting for one day.

For Jesus, they drove the pine box out from the funeral home in the back of the cemetery Groundsman's pickup, because the County wouldn't pay for a big black hearse and a stereo. The guy from the funeral home wouldn't let us tie the box on top of Paul's old black three quarter stretch '66 Cadillac. A dozen or so barely legal American cars with primer or terminal rust rash followed the truck.

As old Sam was mumbling, through whatever it was he was saying about the life of Jesus, and the Jack Daniels that somebody had fed him to get him out here on this frozen day, the rains came.

While he was begging the blessings and forgiveness of a God that I doubt even he believed in, somewhere, down the side of the hill, a two hundred year old maple tree chose that moment to give up it's soul to a shaft of purple lightning.

Cool. The sound of old wood turned into shrapnel sounded like the tirade of a vengeful God that some of us had heard of. Typical.

A couple of people, including Peter the Pyro and Scary Mary, who are both gone now, muttered "fuck you too" under their breath.

123

The nerve to lay those bones in a place so holy as this free from the county shithole grave was too much for the malicious spirit of an old man in heaven who was as bigoted as everybody else in charge of something. The proof that he might be looking in after all proved Jesus had, to some extent, been right about him.

The chrome studs flashed once and the rain came. It came in buckets and barrels. It came and soaked us all to the skin.

Scary Mary, with the rigidity of the righteously pissed off, stood like a statue and barked laughter at the few people who showed discomfort. She'd been with him for two years, off and on, and she wore the old horsehide bike-cop leather that he had always worn.

Somewhere in the pockets she found a joint, more surprising in it's dryness than it's presence in his coat, and lit it. The smoke curled gently blue grey, under the brim of the rumpled hat that she wore to cover her long black hair, and was dissipated by the holes the rain punched in it.

We must have looked sad and pathetic, hard edged posturing, with a soft taint of childhood, in the rain. We felt weak and out of place and we felt as though we would live forever.

The rain stopped falling and old Sam stopped mumbling and we all went our separate ways. A couple of us got straight jobs and cut our hair, some got married or moved away. Almost half of the people who were there that day are dead now and that kind of life is long gone.

Nobody smokes pot anymore.[1] You don't die in cars after too much beer and a fight with your folks or your girlfriend. You don't punch out in a power-shifting fireball at a hundred and ten.
If you're that age now you die in drive by shootings, I guess, even there.

If you were once that age, maybe you sit back and wait for emphysema and arteriosclerosis and a pension and wonder why the kids and all this new music are all so insane. You settle down and get a job and drink a case of Michelob or Bud cans on the weekend watching the game, or maybe go fishing.

---

[1] Originally written at the height of the Nancy Regan "Just say no" drug crusade and prior to any state legalizing medical marijuana or recreational marijuana. Joe was well aware of the uptick in marijuana use since legalization in some states

You learn to stop fighting it all and just try to get hold of a piece of it that you understand, your little piece of the pie.

The Kid's funeral was held, not many weeks later, in the same cemetery, fifty feet away. It rained all that morning too, but early and gentle and when the sun finally came out, things looked cleaner.

Standing there, at the edge of the impossibly dense crowd, listening to Old Sam mumble again, I found a soggy roach, a candle, and a couple of bottle caps next to a cheap little headstone. The name was the one Jesus had been born with.

Some bluejays sat on a branch.

The Kid's mother was heavily tranked, dressed in black, she looked like an overfed raven. She wailed like he never did, and had to be held up by relatives.

Nobody knew what to do with that kind of grief. Few had ever seen it, let alone felt it.

Old Sam and I locked eyes for a moment. Maybe he recognized me, I don't know. I wondered how many of these he had done, and I guess I learned something about him too.

The town is still mostly the same as it was that day, I guess. There are some new faces, and some of the same old ones.

Jack's Donut Shoppe still has a picture on the bulletin board, partially covered in local business cards, left over from some town fight against something the state wanted and eventually got, that shows a cartoon mouse giving the finger to a vicious looking eagle on steep final approach. The mouse knows that it is doomed, but that too is understood.

The picture is titled, "The last great act of defiance".

The town has never changed some of the old blue law rules, so they can't open the shop until seven A.M. The winters are cold and long there, and you learn not to think about it too much. If you hit the place around five thirty or six, you'll find a significant number of the old Townies, the Cops, Politicians and all, sitting around in the dark.

The cash register is off, so you get your coffee yourself and make your own change from a Styrofoam cup on the counter on the honor system. The saying is that if you hang out there in the dark long enough, you'll find out everything in town worth knowing.

Me, I left a long time ago. Physically being there triggered long lost memories. I'm in Colorado these days, where none of this stuff comes back to me.

The thing I recall most clearly about that spring was that the pair of blue jays at The Kid's funeral, the first one of the spring, perched on the rain-wet branch of an apple tree about to bud, and sang.

Poetically speaking, it should probably have been a dove, a lark or the triumphal cry of a hawk or eagle soaring in sunlight high above the clearing clouds.

There are no eagles in Massachusetts. We had blue-jays, they'd just have to do.

When Sheryl asked me what I was thinking, looking out the car window at the rain, I said nothing.

Nothing at all.

Chapter 20

Grandmother and Grandfather Dellea

"Oh Eliot, Eliot-where are you, darling?"
"In America -among the rickety sons and grandsons of the pioneers."
- from God Bless You, Mr. Rosewater, by Kurt Vonnegut, Jr.

"Over the river and through the woods,
to Grandmother's house we go.
The horse knows the way to carry the sleigh..."
- from Over the River and Through the Woods
by Lydia Maria Child

The leaded-gas land-yacht floated East Street on its fat radial white walls as the rain came harder. It slacked as we crossed Thunder Bridge, the deepest black water of the Ipswich, a river even Henry Thoreau didn't like, on the road out of town.

The Ipswich, out by the bridge, always was a good swimming hole, and you get the trick for staying out of the tangled roots near shore early on, or not at all.

The DJ on the radio was one I'd grown up listening to. Same stuff he always played, but he was working at an Oldies station now. I hadn't realized I'd missed him.

We cruised the old high school just for luck or kicks, and tried, vainly, to see if we recognized cars or younger siblings of anybody we knew. The DJ worked his way through "teenage death songs of the early 60's" into a set of Surf Music.

Eight years before, my Aunts and Uncles had gotten together and bought my Grandparents a canoe for their fortieth anniversary, perhaps because they'd once been Idealists of sorts, too. I could believe that, but since they'd been married, in 1943, and raised twelve kids in the best Irish Catholic Tradition, they've only been out to see three movies: African Queen, with Bogie and Katherine Hepburn, some Tough Guy movie with Kirk Douglas, and On Golden Pond, with Henry Fonda and, of course, Hepburn.

I don't know how old I was before I knew anyone my own age who came from an unbroken home, so the whole thing of "the kids" pooling resources to buy the parents an anniversary gift is a little

127

abstract for me. The theme must have, best I can figure, had something to do with helping your Parents find their dreams of youth. Not a problem for the parents of people my age. Either that or it was boats. Everybody likes boats.

"Life is but a dream...", or something. They spent many Summer Sunday afternoons canoeing the old Ipswich.

A friend of some of my Uncles was one Sonny Baron, a Biker who had literally packed up that whole trip when his first kid was born. He'd crated up the motor and some essential parts of his old Harley Knucklehead, bought a van, and promised the wife he wouldn't ride again until motorcycling became safe, or the kid moved out.

That had been some five kids, spaced two or three years apart, ago. By the time that first one was ten Sonny needed a recreational activity. One that would keep him happy, which is to say away from the "*#%!&~@! yard apes", and keep the wife happy, which is also to say, from the other point of view, away from his "drunken, womanizing, goddamned pre-verted, wino buddies".

First Sonny had his van, which he rebuilt from the ground up, starting the year after his youngest was born. 57' Chevy Panel truck with a vacuum progressive Tri-Power, 283, four-speed with overdrive and a Columbia rear axle. Had disc brakes and power steering, too.

The interior was Connolly leather and walnut based on the styling of a Range Rover, and you couldn't eat off of it because that'd make a mess. The only odd things you'd notice about the van were that he'd never actually bothered to completely paint the exterior, so it looked a bit shopworn, and that the radio knob was hot-glued to an Oldies/Classical station. There was a class ring hanging from the knob on a chain.

He took up SCUBA diving for several reasons. His wife liked the idea because he couldn't smoke or drink down there, and nobody cared if he cussed. Sonny liked it because his wife couldn't swim.

He also liked it because when he'd been in high school (at least five kids ago) he'd had access to his father's gleaming gloss black 1958 Cadillac convertible. This was before it was a classic, but it was still a hell of a car.

It seems that, during his Senior year, when Sonny looked, and probably was, a whole lot straighter than when anybody but the other Townies his own age knew him, he was out with this cheerleader, who is now married to somebody or other, and it got fairly debauched out.

128

According to a combination of the various stories, the cheerleader in question either was, or was not, busy somewhere under the dashboard when Sonny closed his eyes for some poignant, but let us say obscure, reason.

The old wooden guardrail on Thunder Bridge didn't offer as much resistance as the Caddy flew through it into the river. The cheerleader and Sonny got out of the open car and they both waded to shore as they watched those rocket-ship taillights sink out of sight in the deep black water.

Sonny said she yelled at him constantly, on the long walk home, that her purse was soaked, and her favorite saddle shoes were ruined for good. And since his class ring, on it's little golden chain had been taken from her neck and hung over a radio knob, during the preceding whatever, so it wouldn't keep hitting him wherever, and since he obviously couldn't drive safely, and was an obviously sick pervert, and so on, and so on, they might as well break up. I have never been able to find out, for sure, who she was, but I suspect she's still in town.

I guess he told his Dad that the car had been stolen. Sonny's Dad beat the literal hell out of him, at least for a while, but Sonny was just so glad, he said, that he could still piss standing up. Nothing could bother him.

After work and weekends, on hot days, Sonny just sits there in his dad's old Caddy, like Dustin Hoffman's character in The Graduate", thirty or so feet down, and relaxes from the pressures of the week. He had a little rubber one-way check valve, mail-ordered from some Diver's supply house, that fits very snugly over the top of a Miller can.

So on Summer Sundays, when I knew the Grandparents were out paddling the canoe, I'd see that old van with the Harley eagle and the "diver down" stickers in the back windows parked out by Thunder Bridge, I'd pull in and stop. Ostensibly to wave to the Grandparents if they should drift by, and sometimes to talk to Sonny. He'd lettered in a couple of sports in High School and was a star early in the career of my high school Wrestling Coach.

I always imagined my Grandparents, in their orange Old Town canoe, picnic basket ever at the ready, trying to act out a late Impressionist painting. My Grandfather rowing like he's sculling for Boston College against Harvard, and Grammy trying to sit still long enough to enjoy the shade of the sun parasol she brought along on these excursions.

Sonny kept a pack of Camel cigarettes on the concrete supports under the new bridge. I could imagine him, like a troll in a kid's story, surfacing, like some fur-bearing tattooed leviathan, beer can in hand, diamond stud in his ear, grinning death's head tattoo on his chest, rising from the depths for a smoke. I could imagine a cordial and shockingly formal greeting to my bewildered Grandparents. Sonny always was a gentleman.

I made the excuse that I stopped by to be civil whenever I knew that this strange conjunction was possible, but I guess the truth of it is that this was a meeting I just didn't want to miss.

As Sheryl and I pulled into the driveway there was not a sound to be heard. No birds in the trees, just the hiss of wet gravel drive under the tires.

Whitish smoke curled from the kitchen woodstove to the branches of the old oak in the backyard. The house had, from the outside, except for the diaphanous yellow and white checked curtains in the sunroom off the kitchen, the look of a Currier & Ives litho: not like a calendar print, more like the engraved steel printing plate. Sheryl and I had time to finish our cigarettes, leaning against the wet car, the rain down to a drizzle, contemplating the house.

Like a Norman Rockwell jack-in-the-box, my grandmother emerged from the back porch screen door, carrying a covered plate of cookies for Sheryl's family, before we could suggest escape to each other, wiping her hands on her apron as though they were birds that would otherwise escape.

She is a sweet lady, and, I think, puzzled by the way things have gone. She weighed a hundred and ten pounds for her high school graduation, in 1939, and twelve children and almost fifty years later didn't mass more than about a Sunday Roaster's worth more than that. She probably hasn't eaten a hot meal, on time and with everyone else, since sometime before V-E day, but, as said, she gave birth, in the grandest Catholic tradition, to a dozen children.

She worries about everyone, and sometimes even understands the problems. The solution is easy, though: Food. From a tax bill to a divorce, from the birth of a grandchild to the death of a friend, the solution was, and always would be food.

Sheryl and I sat at the ancient oak kitchen table, wondered if it was all right to smoke, and had tea. It was Darjeeling that year, hundred-year-old bone china cups and a stoneware pot with small black and white cows on it. They exchanged family and town gossip, my grandmother diverting as much of it as she could my way, to get me up to speed, as the conversation went along, and Sheryl just sort of faded into the background. She could keep the relationships in my family straight as well as I could from knowing me so long, and she was interested anyway.

She says I've got more uncles than Gabe Kaplan, and I think she might be right. Discretely she slips out, leaving me to wade through the legends of relativity. Maybe I should have proposed marriage, so I'd only have to pay half as much attention to my family.

Grammy eventually winds down, and the satisfaction of one of the distant birds coming home to roost, no matter how briefly, comforts her like a forest walk does me. She slows, like a rain turning to a mist on a calm summer night, and slips into the peacefulness of a well-creamed cat.

With Sheryl gone, and my grandmother having reached maternal nirvana, it was decided that I must be tired after my long trip. Well, yes. It seemed that I was. My grandfather and I could try to talk later. I went up to the back bedroom with the personality disorder, and lay down under the fifty pound quilt.

The room had been a nursery when they bought this newer, smaller, house a couple of years ago. It had been, alternately, a library, deep storage, a guest room and an experiment in redecorating that came out as a sort of second floor sitting room with storage boxes. There was an intricate steel frame single bed from the twenties. It had a feather mattress over oiled steel springs, and a cotton and feather quilt. Goose down pillows with heavy lace trimmed Irish linen sheets and pillowcases.

I fell asleep with my glasses on and my old baseball glove sleeping on my chest like a cat. It was after three in the morning, about fourteen hours later, before I remember anything else. I usually only sleep about six or eight hours, and if I wake up in the dark it requires planning.

On the bedside chair was a glass of milk, covered in plastic wrap, and a plate of thick soft chocolate chip cookies, square on the sides from where they'd run together in the pan, and a note that said "Make yourself at home".

I discovered that all my clothes had been stolen as I slept, and flannel pajamas and an unused bathrobe that my grandfather had been given for Christmas 1953 was hung on the back of the chair. My cigarettes, lighter, comb, watch, wallet, change and keys had been laid out upon the doily on the tall maple bureau.

"Why the hell did I bring my house keys?" I thought as I slipped down the front stairs for a smoke in the back yard.

I did some old Tai Chi forms that I have too long neglected, and found that the deliberate, underwater, fluidity fit the place well. I moved as the branches of the trees, and as the waters of the surface of the pool, and periodically looked around to make sure that nobody was watching a fat man in a red silk bathrobe standing under an oak tree and waving like an idiot.

I sat on the maple and wrought iron bench that had been one of their anniversary presents, (forty-five or six, I think) and balanced the cookies and milk on the sundial that had been a different year's gift. I fieldstripped the cigarette, and put the filter in my pocket. Then I realized it wasn't my pocket and walked it out to the driveway.

I took a dawn swim in the pool a bit later, after pacing the neighborhood in a pair of old fur lined moccasins, looking, I'm sure, like Jimmy Stewart on acid, noting only that the mail box looked like it had been backed over a few more times.

I sat in the pine Adirondack chair, at the old wire spool table with the umbrella through the center, and wriggled my toes on the thick wet grass, feeling like a tourist from Kurdistan finding himself magically transported to the Ritz.

The marigolds and peonies were doing nicely. The roses were as good as ever, and that special blue lilac was in almost in bloom. I transferred the cigarette filters to a half-full coffee can of them already behind the garage. The mint was coming in nicely. Good to see that my aunts and uncles had been stopping by.

They've become Third Order Dominicans in the last few years, my Grandparents, and it gives them great comfort and pleasure. It is as close to Clergy as you can get and still be "Of The World" in that system. I'm in my mid to late twenties, and it's hard to explain to them why I'm no longer Catholic. My Grandfather and I could duke it out

132

with our bare fists and brickbats, (and since nearly have) but neither of us would do it in front of my Grandmother.

The sun was up and my grandparents would be up soon, too. There would only be two acceptable excuses for not going to Mass with them: still sleeping from a four-day road trip through hell, or sudden death in the night.

I eased the kitchen door shut behind me and tried to keep my feet quiet as I padded across the living room rug and the kitchen linoleum and then the polished oak of the stairs. The fourth step always squeaks on the right side.

As it turned out, death would have been the only way out of going to Mass.

Chapter 21

Super-cold[2]

"Happy art thou, as if every day thou hadst picked up a horseshoe."
- Henry Wadsworth Longfellow

"It's colder than a witches tit out here."
- Unknown

Going home after a long time causes you to think. At least it causes me to think, Dear Reader. The brain makes some odd associations and you put on some of your old assumptions the way you do a comfortable old jacket on a crisp fall day.

It doesn't matter if it's July or January, the mind comes to rest on some old story and your brain colors all the details back in, the way that a Musician remembers a song.

I remember the trees, and the friends, and the thoughts I felt once in places I haven't seen in a long time.

My family has been staying just ahead of the Boston area's Urban Redevelopment and expansion for about a century now. Just far enough away from the city proper to be able to have a few dogs and occasionally horses. They're as much a part of the bloodline as old cars, and if there isn't a recap tire in the family crest, there ought, at least, to be a thrown horseshoe.

The day we buried Frodo was three weeks into the Super-cold. It was hard on to the middle of March, and it had been below zero since late February. The weather was going to have to break soon.

The damned horse had died in his stall, of course, and the word came through the family grapevine Saturday afternoon that we had to get him in the ground as quick as we could. Somebody else was already taking care of Maggie.

My Aunt Maggie had gotten the horse when she was thirteen or so. All of her siblings had chipped in a bit. As a cure for a budding interest in boys, it had been a pretty good thing. She had tended and

---

[2] A Farmer's Almanac term for a particularly long spell of sub-zero Fahrenheit temperatures.

shown that horse for ten years, and had been married the previous July.

She had married one of the Joyce boys, from out on Joyce Road, and it looked, to my experienced fourteen-year-old eyes, as though they would do all right.

We'd brought the horse down to the Joyce place as a way to get the burden of horse maintenance off of my grandmother. Maggie and Jim had taken an apartment over on the other side of town, and although Frodo was still her horse, her in-laws were doing some of the work for her, as a sort of welcoming to the family.

Between the two families we'd built a sort of barn for the horse out of these big crates that are used to ship stuff from overseas. Each one is half the size of a tractor-trailer sized shipping container. Two or three car-sized boxes, and you've got a pretty fair quick barn.

Now ordinarily, if you have a large animal die on you, the first thing you do is call the Vet or County Animal Health guy and find out what had happened. The Vet comes out and says "yep, your horse is dead", gives you a bill for fifty bucks and goes away.

In our town, things are done on an old fashioned level of expected competency, based, I guess, in some archaic form of Yankee stoicism. There were no other animals in the barn, nor were there likely to be, at that point in the town's zoning regulations.

The town Vet was getting old, and nobody wants to be out in Super-cold if they don't have to. Old Doc Edison said there had been a couple of cases of this particular ailment going around.

"Plant him soon, wear gloves, watch for anything peculiar, and be careful, they have been bloating awfully quick" was what he said.

In the case of the family, my Grandmother called all the boys, the same sons who had pitched in ten years earlier to buy the horse, and all the rest of her children's families. Winter was a pretty slow season, and on the pretext of talking about the dead horse, she got to visit with all of her children, their spouses, and their children.

By late Saturday afternoon she had shaken it down to Artie, Benny, my Father and me. Art made the connection for the backhoe, and the Kramer brothers, Teddy and Eddy would be out about noon Sunday.

There is, in a small town, always the question of rank: ethics and protocols about who you call first in a difficult situation.

In some other similar situation, I guess the first person you call is the Vet. In this case you call the guys who just happen to own the liquor store and the backhoe. They say we Yankees are a practical sort.

I only found out later that Teddy and Eddy had been the first ones called. The Joyce family had anticipated the need.

I later asked why it had been done in that particular rotation, and was told that the Doc couldn't do much for the horse after it was already dead, and the Kramer Brothers would need a day or two to get the "damned machine" plugged in. I'm not sure who told my Aunt Maggie.

The next person in the list was my grandmother, and I'm telling you what happened from there.

The only place I've ever read about Super-cold, and the human body's natural aversion to it, is in an old story by Jack London called To Build A Fire. Normal winter cold is somewhere around zero. Super-cold is unreasonably past that; a spell of five to ten or more below that lasts a week.

It's dry and unreasonably clear. Sound travels a long way. It's too cold to snow. Your spit will freeze in mid-air around thirty below or so.

At that temperature, you are so busy trying to remember what your fingers do, and wondering if your nuts will ever descend from somewhere in the middle of your chest. You don't really have the chance for experimentation.

You try not to go indoors for short periods because the snow blown onto the legs of your jeans will thaw and then refreeze to the consistency of fiberboard when you go back out. Cold vinyl car seats have been known to shatter on contact in that weather.

So not only did I have to go to church with my father and grandparents this morning, but I had to hang out in the middle of the Joyce family's farm while my Uncles pass a pint of Murphy's Irish to work up the courage to decide how to get a full grown, and mostly horizontal, Quarter Horse through a four foot door. Talk about a fun way to spend a weekend afternoon, this beats Creature Double Feature on Channel 56 any time.

Humor is a way to deal with sadness and pain. Anesthesia is another. Most of the women of the family had been able to find enough little yellow tranquilizers to get Maggie able to face anything

136

on television but Westerns. (I'd had no idea that the women of my family had so much in common.)

Maggie, and any of the women, would have been horrified to hear the jokes about chainsaws, food processors, and the going rate at the fast food restaurants that the boys used to get through warming up to the task at hand. I hadn't really anticipated them.

Many of the proposed solutions fell way short of acceptable, and by the time the idea of an experiment in Applied Galvanism using the welder on Artie's pick-up was proposed, it was decided that we might as well get on with it.

Three Pickup trucks idled, their exhaust like breathy mist against the still purity of the cold. The whiskey made another round. I think I was a little drunk.

The backhoe arrived, a homemade affair that used to be most of a 1940's Ford farm tractor. It had leaking seals and pieces of rusting angle iron welded to it in odd places for forgotten reasons; it was chained to (seemed to grow out of) a trailer that looked like it was from the same scrap pile. It was hitched to the back of Eddy's badass four-wheel drive Ford: That big bastard with the 460 and the military axles.

I guess it was necessary to get the Wood chipper jokes ("It slices, It dices....") out of the way before they showed up.

The thing to understand about Eddy is that he doesn't hate you personally; he just dislikes everybody. He's about five and a half feet tall and shaped like an upside down triangle. He owns a mountainous forty-acre section on the edge of town. He was a Tunnel Rat in Vietnam, and, if he can help it, he avoids people. Just stays up there with his guns and his dogs and doesn't come down unless absolutely necessary. Sometimes, when you talk to him, he'll nod and look like he's going to say something, the way some people will when they want to get in the next word, but then he is silent, and you realize he was just waiting for you to stop talking.

His brother Teddy owns the local liquor store and looks like a right side up triangle: Kinda soft at the hips and sloped in the shoulders. He's jovial and will probably end up Mayor if he ever decides he wants to be. They usually helped Artie with his annual 4th of July Pigroast, and last year I was there when they had slaughtered the hog in the garage with a machete and a chainfall.

137

Artie has a "Ford Factory tool" which he is fond of. Most guys have something like this in their toolboxes. It's an eight-pound sledge on a twelve-inch handle. It'll convince almost any stuck anything to move or die trying. He doesn't get to use it much as he'd like, but he keeps it under the seat of his truck just in case.

He knocked the front off the barn with four or five good solid whacks and it fell like a house front in a Buster Keaton Movie.

Sure enough, the dammed horse had begun to bloat.

Doc Edison didn't know what it was yet, but it was going around, and he'd let one of the younger Vets in the area do the autopsy on somebody else's horse.

The paddock was frozen solid to a depth of a foot and a half, but it was fairly smooth and downhill to the spot where Eddy started the hole. Problem was the horse was still, more or less, standing, in the stall, but canted thirty degrees or so to starboard. Removing the wall to the left would mean the cheap little barn would only be on two walls and a roof.

The question was asked of Old Man Joyce, over the CB Radio in one of the trucks "How partial to the barn are ya?"

Old Man Joyce, looking out the kitchen window, came over the radio and said he liked the barn all right, but maybe he'd move it to the other end of the property sometime.

Teddy and Eddy had swapped off on the backhoe, so Eddy could have his turn on the schnapps, and Teddy his turn on the machine. They could work like that for days.

Eddy joined the rest of us, fanned out in front of the (now) three walled barn. The men, of whom I was now one, as shown by the pint of Irish in my hand, looked from each other to the horse.

The horse looked back.

We didn't say anything.

The horse didn't either.

There was no sound, except for the distant cars on the highway and the snarling of the little hand-made backhoe.

A grin spread over Eddy's bearded face like a Spring Grizzly waking from his long winter's nap in front of a Bennigan's buffet table.

I guess I should have guessed by the fact that that Eddy was drinking Schnapps and breathing through his mouth (to avoid ice crystals in the nose), and by the fact that he looked happy, that the solution was going to be an original one.

He loped down the hill, like the aforementioned bear closing on the smoked salmon, and skidded to a halt next to the backhoe. Through some sort of sibling communication, or merely the urge to swap backhoe for booze, Teddy yielded the machine.

No sooner was he aboard than the little dinosaur began to rev higher than I'd imagined it could, raised it's bucket like putting your fist in your armpit, backed across the flat and took a good run on the hill.

Amazingly, Eddy got it to within a little distance of the crest of the hill in two tries and sunk the bucket into the backside of a pine stump just over the top with enough force to lift the big back wheels clean off the ground.

He looked at the horse, the horse looked at him.

He stepped down from the little red tractor and paced the little red barn the way Minnesota Fats paces around a pool table.

"Sure we shouldn't just dig a barbecue pit?", said Artie, sounding dubious.

"Schnapps", said Eddy to Teddy.

"I got some marshmallows and hamburger buns back at the house", said Benny.

"Hammer", said Teddy to Artie.

"Chain", said Eddy to me, and I went and got it from the truck.

Eddy slipped into the stall, past the listing horse, and jumped up to hit the corners of the three-walled barn. My Dad had that bemused look that he gets when other people are doing or saying weird stuff.

The impacts of the unpatented Ford Factory Adjustment and Calibration Device against the walls of the tiny barn sounded like shotgun blasts in the cold of the afternoon.

"Move", said Eddy to Artie, emerging from the barn.

"Wha...", said Artie, as the little backhoe began to scream.

Eddy engaged the wheels before they were even on the ground, and got them there by abruptly pulling up the bucket. The wheels began to spin, and then the tractor began to buck before they began to catch. Up, and over the last foot of the hill, hang a right, with the arm straight out in front. When he stopped, the bucket of the backhoe was all the way inside the barn, and in between the highest side of horse and the wall, with a few inches to spare either way.

The Motor revved, the dead horse stared, and my father and uncles looked nervous.

With the sweet precision that only the truly talented can ever hope for, Eddy popped the lever that controlled the bucket, causing it to pop the roof straight up and over the back wall of the barn. It folded all the way over and separated from the side walls, which obligingly fell straight out.

The weight of the horse against the unsupported stall divider had gone over and the horse with it. A perfect sled.

"Schnapps", he said to his brother.

A dead horse is big, but a little more fragile than you'd think. Fortunately it didn't break.

It was obvious that it was going to be all down hill from there, so Eddy let my uncles have the honor of folding up the rest of the barn, and attaching the chain to old Frodo's sleigh.

My uncle Artie, being who he is, eyed the horseshoes, with an eye toward household decoration. The Brothers Kramer said nothing as passed the schnapps back and forth while they watched them work.

When it was ready, Teddy climbed aboard the little engine that might, and, not willing to be out done by his "Baby Brother", lined up Frodo's last ride.

He backed and filled with the little tractor until he was just down the hill, with the chain hooked to the bucket and the now horizontal barn wall. I could see that he was going to get the wood, carrying the horse, to slide down the hill, and I figured that he knew more about it than I did. The horse, who lay there on his side as if running on the wrong plane began to swell even further, and the gas caused him to look like he might be grinning.

Just as quick as can be, Teddy jerked the chain back, and cut hard to the left, out of the path of the advancing former steed.

CRuuuunnk, went the wood over the pine stump.

SSSSHHHHHHHhhhhhh went the sled down the hill.

Boooonng, went the chain when it reached the end of it's slack, and Crrrr went the body of the horse as it ground to a halt some five feet from the hole, off the front end of the sled, with his hooves in the wrong direction.

"Shhhhhiit!", said the assembled group as a whole.

The choices from here were not plentiful. The danger of accidentally tearing the horse open if we had to drag it across the ground was pretty high.

If we could get it four feet closer, we could just slip it into the hole and go home, but the rigor had left the horse, and it was like trying to get a full waterbed to the other side of the room.

"Teddy", said Eddy, "you missed."

"Ayyuh," said Teddy, who was studying on the problem from the seat of the little red tractor, "I know".

Silence ensued for one of those minutes that felt like an hour, and in it we heard the sound of a car door closing, close up to the house, which was out of sight over the little hill. Benny ran intercept, and the rest of us thought on the problem for a bit.

What we finally settled for was to roll the horse one half of a turn, so that the legs would at least be a bit closer, and perhaps we could get another grip with the chain from the other side of the whole and drag him in from there. We put a board between each of the legs and the ground, but it was sort of like trying to use leverage on a block of tofu.

Finally, by getting the backhoe bucket right up against the horse, we were able to get the legs to come up a bit, and when they got up to just short of the center point, with each of us holding on to a corner of the horse, and the bucket under the belly, it rolled. But since all the rigor had gone out of it, it kept rolling, and the head came around and pinned Artie to the frozen ground, nearly knocking him into the hole, as it rolled over him.

The horse rolled right on past it's other side and the legs splayed out in all directions, and went right on past it's center point and down into the hole on it's back. The feet stuck straight up about a foot above ground.

To use the word "thunk", or to even attempt to relate the sound of eight hundred or so pounds of half frozen, half gaseous dead horse rolling over an uncle, and down into a frozen hole in the ground is to admit that the language has it's limitations. I'm okay. with that.

What gave us a problem was that the horse had landed with his legs straight up in the air, directly in the middle of the hole. It was not wide enough to lay the horse on its side, and not deep enough to have the horse be upside down. We looked over our shoulders to see if anybody was watching.

Eddy looked at Teddy and said "Not much of a hole, ya know".

As we were trying to figure out how to deal with this, we heard, damned near simultaneously, the sounds of the car door back over the hill closing, and the sound of the gas finally escaping the horse. The idea that Maggie had gotten someone to bring her out to say last parting words to her friend Frodo was definitely the scariest part of what was going on.

The closest I can get to explain that sound is to say that it was like thirty seconds of the biggest whoopee cushion you ever heard. The legs folded down and deflated.

Artie, realizing that the smell wasn't going to rise during the cold, ventured a little closer to re-examine the aesthetic possibilities of one of those horseshoes, with an eye toward household ornamentation.

I suppose I should have been the one to warn Bennie about tossing that cigarette into the grave as he came back over the hill. Or maybe I should have warned Artie to step back, before the blue flame took the furthest half-inch off of his beard. From the position that everybody else was in when it happened, they were caught between the two options as well.

"Schnapps?" said Eddy and Teddy.

Artie, with his eyebrows singed, and his beard now somewhat shorter, hiked up to his truck as we all stood staring. He returned with a flat-bar and a hacksaw, and commenced to remove the shoes. They came off easily.

The hole got filled in, and my Dad and I have never spoken of the day we buried Frodo. And I've never told anybody but you this story until now.

Yes, there are a few "lucky horseshoes" floating around the family.

Chapter 22

Revisiting Dad

"When you comin' home, Dad
I don't know when
but we'll get together then..."
- from Cat's in the Cradle by Harry Chapin

My father lived in an 18th century tree house, at that time. At least he called it a tree house. In reality it was a small apartment in a converted attic above a two hundred-fifty-year-old tavern in a microscopic New Hampshire town.

There is a straight white stair that runs between the house and a fat maple. The tavern is a house now, and has been for at least a hundred years. For my grandparents it might as well be a flophouse above a strip joint in Boston's legendary, and now deceased, Combat Zone, but they'd never say so out loud.

The tavern had been a mail stop on the old Northern Route of the Boston Post Road, and it overlooks a small triangular Parade Ground intended for militia practice. There is a round covered well with a trim shingled roof, but no cannon. He's been here for years, and says he'll never come back down to Massachusetts.

Maps, for my grandfather, are read after Mass, not because Sunday drives in the country have been out of fashion since the oil embargo of '73, but because he remembers and keeps custom. Maps are read, formally, because my grandfather must, as is the way of these things, find a best direct route. Crows ask him how to get around.

In New England the archetypal directional query response is supposedly "You can't get there from here", drawn out so long that the sentence can take thirty seconds to be fully spoken. That's the popular myth, as tourists from Jersey and points South would have it, but the truth is simply that the day just ain't long enough to describe all the options.

Maps are used to shrink the distance down to about 40 miles as the crows fly. The drive between the two houses used to take me well over two hours.

I'm a mailbag in the back of a small and modern Buick that my grandfather ordered from the factory with a manual transmission and no radio. Like the Fairmont before that, and all but the Buick just before that. He used to drive no heater-no radio Chevys, and my Dad was a Ford Man. You can't get cars without heaters and floor mats anymore, so they are allowed to stay, grudgingly. The old Post Road, in Spring, is as pretty as that vague New Hampshire-Massachusetts border can get. More than I can describe.

My grandfather, as is the custom, waits in the car, while my grandmother comes up to see the place, and maybe visit a bit because my Dad's truck is in the dooryard.

As usual, it's his other truck, and he is at work. There is a note and a twenty-dollar bill, and the keys to the truck, sitting on the kitchen table.

The apartment is, on the surface, neater than I've ever seen him keep one, so I wonder who the current romantic interest is. My grandmother can assess a room faster than an IRS Field Rep, and I see puzzlement there too. The ashtrays are empty, the books and magazines neat on their shelves. There are no dishes in the sink, the Craftsman toolbox he uses for a coffee table has been waxed recently; the anvil in the corner has a plant sitting on it. An actual live plant. It is kind of surreal for both of us.

She doesn't check drawers and cupboards, I think, because she had children at home all through the Fifties, Sixties and Seventies, and she seems to have decided that there are just some things about your children that you don't want to know.

She places the cake that she has brought on the worn but clean orange Formica counter, knowing that bringing the glass plate and cover back will make either my father or me come down to see her. We say our good-byes, and confirm that I'll be back before I leave the area.

After a cursory investigation she closes the door slowly but firmly on her way out. It feels like she's locking me in, and I wait to hear the car downstairs before I move.

Quiet. Blessed quiet. There is only a clock radio for music, and I try to hunt up a good rock station that had disappeared in my absence. There is a classical station playing Bach, the good solid stuff. No spider-web waltzes today.

There is a can of coffee in the cabinet and half a loaf of Roman Meal wheat in the fridge. It's nice to be able to count on things.

The note says that the truck, which is newer than the last one I remember, gets it's best mileage between fifty five and seven, and that he's on the road, running between Portland, Maine, New Jersey, and Conestoga, New York.

There is a television, and a fridge with eggs and grape jelly. A polystyrene dozen-egg carton, with eight eggs used and the shells put back in the box. Forgot about that habit, always fucking hated it.

I madk fried egg sandwiches with the last of the eggs, drink a pot of coffee, and browse the books. Assorted paperbacks from truck stop wire racks, a bible, some trucking magazines, a couple of Playboys and a copy of Whitman's Leaves Of Grass that I sent him from somewhere on the road one year when I happened to remember.

There is a weatherman on a small channel up there who sounds like, as my buddy Tony once said, a gay vampire on speed. "Gooooooood EEeeeevning", in-fuckin-deed.

I hadn't thought this through, but somehow the plan had just come together. Somehow I'm here. I missed a couple of connections, and ended up sitting in my father's house imagining conversations. What the hell are we supposed to talk about if he should show up? It had been five years and it hadn't really occurred to me that we'd have to re-meet each other.

I investigate some more, and find that, with the exception of that damned trick with the eggs the place is as spotless as possible.

I'm supposed to be in Montpelier at two o'clock tomorrow afternoon and I have no idea what to do in the meantime. I walk around the little triangular town green, designed for militia practice back when it was still a British Colonial province. Look into the well.

Hike two miles into town and buy some eggs and a dollar notebook to begin this project in. I make fun of the weather guy on one of the three available television channels, and switch back and forth between Rooster Cogburn and The Treasure of Sierra Madre on the other two. Sometimes you just get lucky I guess.

At ten thirty I heard a Detroit Diesel on a thirteen speed clear the small hills near the town center over a mile away. The driver is shifting without the clutch, balancing RPMs and speed, hitting the little rises perfectly, a skill almost none of the people driving trucks today even know about.

So this is how we'll see each other after the intervening couple of years? Well shit, ain't that a switch. I get out the things to make coffee, tuck in my shirt, and go down the stairs.

We hold our coffee cups in our right hands. Thick mismatched mugs, with hands wrapped most of the way around.

The thing about my father that I always see are his hands. They are huge and horribly distorted. Knurled like tree roots. Hard as stone.

Mine have been broken and cut a few times, but these days the worst I get are splinters, paper cuts and cigarette/pen calluses. Soft, by comparison.

His hands are the size of old fashioned baseball gloves, cracked and hard and regularly oiled. The fingers have been re-arranged every time they get mangled by a stubborn machine, the skin turns dry-out white from fuel oil or the methanol you pour into frozen winter air brakes, red from scrubbing, brown from sun through a windshield. It is an erosional/growth process that has been going on since before I was born. My hands look like his would have had he gone straight. His look like heavy-gauge articulated parts of a diesel.

The old man holds his cigarette like a tool, like a Glazier folds a short glass-cutter when working on heavy-stock Bullseye, it rests even, and precisely parallel to the tabletop, trapped precisely between the first knuckles of his right hand. The smoke of his Lucky Strike rises toward the ceiling in an uninterrupted gray-blue line. I try to do the same, but don't have his stillness.

We look at each other's eyes, and see reflected back the same gray washed blue. The creases and furrows are almost the same in some places.

There is a little more gray in the beard, and the old scar on the right cheek still shows through. He can, I guess, see something in me too, but I have no idea what.

We can only appraise and never speak of what is real: it is not done. We talk of things rather than Ideas. We speak of goals rather than wishes. Objectives rather than dreams, because it is a language we have both learned over time for different reasons, but here and now they are almost the same thing.

We drink our coffee, I with sugar, and my spoon in the cup: he with his milk and sugar. Sometimes we're Enemies, Father and Son. There are many things we, both probably, wish could be said. They can't yet, and maybe never will.

146

It's been a couple of years, but we're both too tired and awkward to talk, though we'd like to if we knew how.

He takes the bed, and I take the couch, twenty feet away. We lay there in the night, listening to each other breathe.

After a long time I say, quietly to hedge the bet, "Dad?".

"Yea?," he says, out there in the darkness.

"I forgot," I say simply, "coffee keeps me awake nights".

We laugh well, and shortly go to sleep.

The morning is crisp and clear, like there is a law in the whole New Hampshire and Vermont area that permits only two kinds of weather for the returning Prodigal Son: Andrew Wyethe light on clear fields or murderous snowstorms that can kill you at the end of your driveway. Fortunately, I got the better.

The old man is gone when I wake at Eight, nearly the crack of noon by local standards. His note is back on the table, and another ten has been added to change from the initial twenty. I have no idea what that means.

Beneath the earlier note, in his lapsed Catholic school handwriting, that makes the letter "T" an inverted four, is the explanation that he had to go to Bangor. When I get back down in a couple of weeks he'll show me the possible trucks he's got lined up. In the meantime I'm to make myself at home with his Ford, and keep it between 55 and 57 on the highway or, as the note says, "you can hear the gas-money clattering out the tailpipe".

I gather up my bags, clean up the kitchen, check the oil in the truck, thump all the tires, note the mileage and hit the road again, this time driving. I hit the Dunkin' Donuts at Epsom Circle and roll up 93 toward Vermont in the epitome of rural Yankee style.

I did think about hiding the bumper sticker: "If it ain't broke, Don't Fix it!" but it wasn't my truck.

Reconciling myself with town names like White River Junction and Royalton may not mean anything to you if you've never been up that way, but if you have, they are magic on the tongue and on the memory. White River, or just "Junction" as it is known to some, is the state border crossing and where the hills change dramatically.

It looks, as always, like somebody built it to specs derived from the side of a maple syrup can.

Vermont! Somehow I made it. Sweet Green Vermont.

Home of the Sugar Bush. Home of hillsides that, every Autumn, bloom brighter than any Artist can capture. Rock maple and birch, hardwoods and Mast Pines.

Home of three hundred year old farmhouses, hot maple sugar spread right on the woodsy snow, perfect town squares, freezing crystal creeks, the Green Mountain Boys and all the rest of that.

Now to see if it was worth it.

Chapter 23

Life Kits

"They got an apartment with deep pile carpet
and a couple of paintings from Sears..."
- from Bottle of Red, Bottle of White, by Billy Joel

One of the best friends I ever had was a guy named Tony. We went through High School together as satellite members of the same crowd, but never got to be really tight until Senior Year. We'd sort of known each other from around for three years, but that year really sucked for both of us. And three years was the longest I had been in any one school.

You see, my Dad really blew it, and ended up down at the VA Hospital that Fall, and I got clocked with double bronchial pneumonia. Tony's Mother got Cancer of the lung, and Tony had some asswipe in Papa's T-bird lock up the brakes in front of his bike, which broke both his legs, his right arm, cracked his pelvis, and pissed off his girlfriend by nearly killing her at the same time.

You could say we had a lot to talk about that year.

He was always a Faceman, the good-looking one who never had to learn much about playing well with others, while I have always come across as sort of Thug-like.

When he was in the hospital, doing six weeks hanging from ropes and learning to like Demerol, we had a lot to talk about. Tony, aside from being pretty good with his bike, was into Karate and Ballet, and he had some adjustments to make. It was me he wanted to talk to, so I hung around and talked with him when I could.

Most of the time was spent running different scams on the Med staff. When they told him that television was going to be five bucks a day we found a portable battery rig, and I'd drop off a couple of packs of Duracells every few days.

When I trucked his bike up to a shop to have the frame straightened and the rest of the repairs done, I brought the sissybar, some bolts, and the mangled highway pegs over to the hospital.

I think the Doctor believed him when he said he wanted some of the metal from his bike to go into the pins and screws they were using to nail him back together. He didn't buy the bit about occupational therapy, when we claimed to be bringing the motor in next week.

Eventually they relented on the television thing and gave it to him for free, to keep him from being a revolutionary symbol of antiestablishmentarianistic revolt.

By the time his three months were up, and he finally got out of there, we were having wheelchair drag races down in the basement, featuring one hand, two hand, and electrically powered classes among the patients.

Most of this was just an extension of our High School Hallway Rap, which was sort of a mass psych-out, just for the fun of it.

In a class-conscious preppie school you get a kind of inherent wish to affirm your station. When the clean-cut, blow-dried, well-dressed Dancer/Karateka and that big hoodlum with the denim jacket and work boots began hurling racial, ethnic, ancestral and sexual pejoratives at distances of a hundred yards, there was going to be a fight. Elementary, even in High School.

When it got down to fifty yards the invectives dealt with bestiality, incestuous behavior, rampant and flagrant homosexuality, and the potential number of infectious diseases the other had contracted on their last tour of duty as mosh-pit floor-licker and draft-not-bottled livestock inseminator. Speculations on how many dozens of coins they had earned in those Tijuana back alleys. As Tijuana was three thousand miles away, we were basing the pejorative speculation on rumors.

By the time we had it down to thirty feet, everyone in a given hallway would have stopped pretending to find their locker contents so interesting, and stared openly at a death in the making.

At twenty feet the pejoratives left off any pretense of joviality at all, as fighting postures were adopted and the insults went from the speculative to the direct, and the Hood and the Preppie were about to spill some serious blood on the floor.

And at ten feet it got really insulting.

The standard set of variations from there would involve all the postures preparatory to the teenaged male fighting ritual, sometimes known as "Push-Push". We'd close the gap fast, and then pause for as long as we felt the crowd could hold still for it....

Then we'd either do the semi-passionate open-hand-over-the-other-guy's-mouth dip-kiss, or the conversational "Hey, did you catch that movie on TV last night?" while watching the let-down crowd out of the corners of our eyes.

With the exception of the time the Administration got that search warrant for my super-glued and balloon-filled locker, or the time I made sixty bucks on that Haircut-and-Suit bet, it was the best time I had in school. Tony's best time had something to do with rustling livestock into a third floor administrative office as a diversion for the roofing of a Volkswagen, if I remember it right. Apparently cows can't descend stairs.

We were a couple of normal high school boys, who had been sent in different costumes by central casting.

Over the intervening years we'd gone down different career paths. He had taken up Nursing after getting so much direct experience with hospitals, I had wandered around doing all sorts of jobs, from clerking for the IRS to fixing beer trucks and building houses.

He married one of my ex-girlfriends, and I chased one of his to Colorado thinking I was in love with her. When I got the wedding invitation I was living in my Chevy in Boulder Canyon, having tossed away the East Coast, and the whole old life, allegedly in pursuit of this girl.

It turned out to be a really intensive way to quit drinking, snorting, and eating steadily. I like to think I learned a lot of lessons. Believe me, I don't ever want to have to learn them again.

Tony was allowed to keep most of his until his wife had him busted and detoxed for punching her out about two years down the line.

The way I saw the thing, in my visit with the lovely and picturesque young couple, just before their "first Christmas together as a married couple", during the Winter I wimped out on Colorado, they had been roadkilled by the "Life Kit" delivery truck.

Now maybe I'm a bit cynical, and I've been told that I'm as much fun in a relationship as a dog-shy horse at a foxhunt, but I've seen the Life Kit take out some of the people I thought had decent sense.

Marriage is one thing, and I respect it so much I've never tried it.[3] The Life Kit is a different sort of thing, a sort of subgroup of accumulated Consumerist desires, usually justified by a marriage license in a frame from a department store. It tends to hit young marrieds in the form of the wedding-gift wagon train.

The first is usually a set of silverware or a set of "fine china", it doesn't matter which set comes first.

As the bug caught Tony and the lovely Mrs. Tony (formerly "Lovely Lisa", also known as "Luscious Lisa", AKA "Lascivious Lisa" and "that hot little blonde in the leather mini") the first acquisition was a Diningroom Set. Immediately followed by cutlery, crockery (both ceramic and the all important stainless steel), cookery, electric and manual kitchen utensils, and naturally, glassware.

Flowing organically from there are the microwaves, three crock-pots and two toasters that came in with the wedding loot, and a spice rack with an instruction book that they bought themselves.

These were only the Kitchen Implements, and barely hint at the "Home Entertainment Center". It seemed a bit pretentious, to me, to refer, always in full capital letters, to the particle-board shelving unit where the television, with attendant VCR, stereo from Sears, and full cable service resides, but who am I to judge? I had no idea their home was bored.

In the case of Tony and Lisa, basking in the glow of their recent haul was not enough. They seemed to feel that being married entitled them to be the people that they had seen on television. Like TV Dinners, life came prepackaged. Ready to Wear.

A desire to get a pet, in preparation for those kids they were supposed to begin producing, turned into a thousand dollar investment in a fish tank full of rare tropical exotics whose names were immediately forgotten.

They bought a female Bluepoint Siamese kitten for $600.00 and thwarted the reason for the price by having her fixed the first time she went into heat.

That Winter I was working as a Baker at Au Bon Pain, a fast-food French restaurant. They were pronouncing the name in

---

[3] The author was single at the time this book was written.

protracted phonetic American, with a long O, and I was "Going Tharn"[4].

Like Mr. Adams rabbits, I could see myself, losing my mind in the little store-front food stall. Getting small and furry. Imagining my teeth happily munching away at tiny carrots, my glasses bobbing up and down on the end of my nose, just waiting for that shining wire. I imagined that I would be "Going Tharn" two ways: slowly, and then, of course, all at once....

I stopped hanging out with them, during my short visit back, because they were drinking a fifth of booze a night and taking pictures of each other "making our first pot-roast as a married couple".

I'll give them this, they clung to it tenaciously.

Tony and I ran into each other, just before I left for good and came back to Colorado. He had bought a 16 foot powerboat, a set of rods, and had begun amassing tackle at a rate that must have had clerks at K-mart and Abercrombie & Fitch laughing until they wet their pants. He told me he "was a Fisherman now", and he sounded like he believed it.

Eventually the money ran out, and paying American Distress with Monstercard, so you can get a cash advance to pay the other one, hardly ever gets you very far except very far into the hole. You end up wishing for nuclear holocaust around every 14th of the month, just so you don't have to pay the bills.

The phone went off and on like a light, the lights did the same. They ducked the landlord. When booze got cut from the budget in favor of one of the ill-fated car loans, it got rough. The framed marriage license and the silver-plated wedding cake tray got thrown in anger. China plates loaded with Chef Boyardee Ravioli missed each other in mid-air and splattered against the leased couch. You get the idea.

I didn't hear from either of them for a couple of months, by which time I'd gotten myself a solid place to live back in Boulder, and Lisa called me long distance, looking for Tony because she wanted to throw him in jail.

---

[4] A phrase from the old Watership Down novel to explain what happens to a rabbit when it stops in the middle of the road transfixed by the onrushing headlights of a car.

Tony wrote me from jail a month after that, because he had apparently shot and killed the satin-sheeted waterbed with a portion of his newly acquired gun collection.

They were both fucking their AA Sponsors. And then Lisa was fucking both their AA Sponsors. And then Tony wrote me from jail, just after the DTs wore off.

The Divorce Set, alimony and acrimony, came soon after, and I was thankful there hadn't been kids. I didn't hear from either of them for a couple of years.

I never found out who got custody of the cat.

Chapter 24

Welcome to Academia

"I'm quite contented to take my chances
against the Guildensterns and Rosencrantzs..."
- from How Could You Want Him
(When You Know You Could Have Me)? by the Spin Doctors

"This place can be wondrous strange at times..."
-Winnie The Pooh

Downtown Montpelier glows like a Taoist's electric emerald in the heart of a gentle forest.

It isn't a gentle forest, none are, but the land knows that you'd better respect it, and here the people listen, so the forest can be considered gentle.

There is no fuckin' golden-arched restaurant, and this is the last State Capitol holdout. There's a Ben & Jerry's store with flying cow mobiles, wings outstretched like mutant dairy crows (don't ever stand under a flying cow!), and the place is decorated in festive balloons, and a style that could be titled "Very Late Enviro-Hippie". It's beautiful, even without comparison to it's plasti-clad nemesis.

I bop the downtown like ol' Sherlock on his coke, superatenuated, like Kerouac on his first day in Denver, lookin' at all the toys and accouterments of paradise: Vermont Airtight Stoves, maple sugar candy, books. It ain't always Paradise, as the Winters testify, and every so often the river here reminds you that it's alive, but still...

The city had flooded out just the month before, but was dredging out nicely: there were numerous sales on slightly waterlogged books.

There are about a dozen bookstores (at least one with it's own press) in downtown Montpelier.

They've got a converted movie theater that still shows movies and also rents the best selection of Art Films and Classics and New

Stuff to get you through Winter that you could possibly hope for north of 47 degrees, anywhere this side of Vancouver. It is painted a distinctive chocolate color that at least one person referred to as "Savoy Brown".

If you spend enough time in a place like this, larger places stop making sense.

A gingham woman in a bookstore offered me a dose of Liebovitz and a draught of Poe as a specific against all ills. A Jeffersonian Yeoman at the sub-shop folds his laptop computer and freely discusses with me various aspects of a book of Yeats' poetry in relation to post-Industrial rural acclimatization: says Edward Abbey is a natural extension. A 50 year old Cowgirl from New York City takes my picture as I sit at a sidewalk cafe table: She says I look like part of the local color.

Six more bookstores, a finest kind bagel bakery, no McDonald's, and fewer cops than they have people who've thrown barn raisings. I could be local color if they'd ask me.

I sit at a sidewalk table, well beneath the recent waterline, with a gray rain threatening overcast, happily munching an Elite chocolate bar. That, and a cup of poisonously strong espresso, an International Herald Tribune and the world is heaven.

Elite: Israeli chocolate. A green wrapper shot through with gold stripes, and ornamented with a picture of a stone house and a cow, mountains and trees, and it's even Kosher for Passover. I'm not Jewish, but Kosher can't hurt. The dietary rules of the Middle East grew out of necessity. They make them in Ramat-gan, Israel: a place that exists miraculously for more reasons than good chocolate. It's oddly emblematic of life, this chocolate made in a warzone. And nobody tried to wrap it in polystyrene, either.

Finally, it is time. Half an hour before the appointed time I let the Ford with the "If it ain't broke, don't fix it!" bumper sticker escalate me up the hill.

The buildings of the College itself nestle perched at the top of the hill like the castle in Teike's old tale.

To some, scattered far upon the mid-west table top, it must look be the ancestral Bates' manse. For me it winks Vacancy, room for one more.

The roommate is a Celtic/Hindu Carpenter from Toronto, and the Professor I pick for my Mentor holds an auction license that he says he got in the pursuit of the perfect omelet. The roommie says he'd wondered if I wouldn't snore so loud. I tell him I'll try. He accepts this. If I fail he doesn't tell me.

Two weeks in the northern palace of literary heroism, which, in fact, lends itself, in name, word, and deed, if not in spirit, to a better financially backed military academy that is in dire need of a claim to offer some Liberal Arts. Besides, it's fun to watch the Cadets when you say "Liberal Arts".

Among the celebrants, postulants, fellow travelers and Liberal Artists are fine folk like:

Betty, a housewife from Chicago who'd love the Naked Beat Angels, and swears they'd go over well at tea.

Sparks who throws intellectual fire in a Feminist co-op theater off the coast of Washington State.

Arthur, originally from Wisconsin, who's moved into my old Andover neighborhood and is practicing the Yankee Lock-jaw accent. He means well, and I think it upsets him that I was in a kids bowling league at the place around the corner from him that is now a brew-pub.

Marie, the quiet and intense dark-haired Theosophist from Philadelphia, who carefully explains the humor in Marcel Duchamp's use of phonetic multi-letter French puns,

Claire, a rural artist, who has a neon-painted cow skeleton recovered from a sinkhole in her Pennsylvania farm backyard strung on wire from her front porch to a friendly branching poplar tree (and more surprisingly, a picture of it with her),

Lewis, who is a Major in the Salvation Army, and is batting out his degree studying Robert Bly.

Caroline, the Secret Lesbian, who hijacks me late one night to cruise around Vermont backroads listening to "Women's Music". She thinks I'm the only one who knows she's Gay, and can't figure out how I know. During the second week she appears at my door late one night and says, desperately, "I need you". I sputter and she smiles and calls me a moron. She'd been talking to a couple of the Cadets, and needed to find a human male to discuss politics.

There's the young Aussie Hemingway who lives in an Outback rolligon trailer and has mescaline dreams of leather winged apparitions sent by the friendly Abo's down the road.

Alex, who, after studying Plato and Aristotle's epiphanies, is going to read for the Law next year.

Donna, who is over fifty, and keeps her PowerMac in the back of her fat black Mercedes panzerwagen and writes good poems about generic and superfluous life. For the first minute I knew her I was afraid that she might be generic and superfluous life.

And there is Leon, the old campus security guard, a "local" whose, soon to be fatal, cranial melanomal lump makes him spout obscenities, even in the midst of mostly liking these weird and confusing kids whose median age is thirty.

A brass plaque at College Hall, the first major building on campus, more than a hundred and a half years old, memorializing the half dozen former names of the place, reads:

> "Theirs was the spirit of honest inquiry,
> the spirit of hospitality to new light
> and truth from any quarter, the spirit
> of understanding which sees all life is
> one and that every truth must live
> at peace with every other...
> ...A spirit that made a great school."

The motto of the Military side of the place is "I will try", which, if you ask me, is all anybody can hope for.

Two weeks of orgiastic intellectualization: Ragus and readings, art exhibits and long Existentialist conversations. There are still books I was told about then, that I still haven't read.

Sparks and I discuss the nature of anti-feminine pejoratives in the language in a public enough way that people are waiting for a fight.

I say "Yea, it is a bitch", right on her cue, and she tries to concuss me with a dinner roll. Later she gets a similar one from me.

Good books are discussed openly, rather than by furtive nerds.

Pieces of poetic reference, and illusory allusion are bandied about like Frisbees in a park, and nobody threatened my life for punning or reading (alright, patching and borrowing and making up) a survey of the moment as a noxious tone poem at the Tuesday night Ragu.

Ragu or Raga? Last I heard the official title of the function was under investigation by a group intent on proper Vedic translation, and a desire not to sound like a spaghetti sauce.

I made some good friends there, and got an inkling that, in spite of fifteen years of previous formal education, that Education encourages good thinking. Well, that and the fact that they tolerated my bullshit.

There are thousands, perhaps millions of us, out there. In the small towns whose names are only known by the locals, and we're there in the midst of those famous megalopolic cities.

There are people who are awake inside. Because of their failure, our failure, my perceived failure, to be able to articulate, because of restricted language or lack of an audience to go beyond that veil, some of us die never having tried.

I never imagined I could actually publish a book until I was twenty-five, though I've read constantly since age five. I'm still not sure this one will ever see the light of day.

I'm supposed to be a Truck Driver, and live very near to where I was born. Truck Drivers are, from what I've seen, not supposed to write poetry. Even if this book that you hold in your hands is the biggest mental masturbation of the twentieth century, at least it got done, and I have some inkling of what a completely incompetent jerk I can be. I failed to be a Truck Driver.

Am I part of the most significant literary movement since Pound hitchhiked to Venice, or am I just fucking around? I'm not sure, but I'm trying. If we all did, then perhaps the world would not hurt us all so much.

Early on a sunny Vermont morning I go to the woods to find a place to meditate. Down the hill behind the College, there is what you could only call "A Fort". That's what we called them when I was a kid. It is a reminder of our collegiate paramilitary brethren who've recently evacuated this bivouac in favor of the other campus and leaving the hippies the hell alone.

It is made out of hatcheted and bow-sawn pine saplings at horrible expense to board footage, and the place is half swathed in liberated tarpaper, and fallen shingles and covered in browned pine boughs. Temple to the Tom Sawyer dreams of the boys who grew on tales of a Mars that looked like central Iowa/Illinois in the twenties.

The primal stone fire ring in the sodden center holds a water-swelled book on logic so obtuse and abstract as to be silly, and a copy of the Wall Street Journal dated three weeks before. There is a school pennant, and other tribal memorabilia that, it seems, just would not catch fire. I open the paper and can still smell the naphthalene from a can of lighter fluid. There is a cuff-link and a crumpled letter of acceptance from an ivy-league school to a cadet with a hyphenated name. The initials on the Letter and the cuff-link don't match, and I wonder how many participated in the ritual.

After thorough investigation, and some time spent communing with the trees, I climb back up the hill, and rejoin the festival of ideas, thoughts and poetry.

In the midst I pause, take a time out as only a Roman at the orgy, or a former Catholic boy, when he's having a good time being smart, could do. I pause to make a couple of phone calls to re-affirm that the old worlds are still out there spinning, and still hold sway, if for no reason other than to keep from being swallowed in the maelstrom of mindfulness.

My Dad's answering machine is on.

My roommate Maryanne has had her ex-boyfriend staying at the house and plastering the spare bedroom. He'd been sleeping on my futon. While he was working she went camping and took my futon. The futon was killed in a horrible and tragic tent fire. She hoped I wouldn't be pissed because she had gone camping with fifteen of her friends on the advice, more or less, of her Shrink who was going to up her Lithium dosage, and perhaps cross-prescribe Prozac. If I was pissed she'd buy me a new one anyway when I got back, so I wasn't pissed, was I? etc. etc...

160

My Grandparents were fine, and Grammy said that my father had located a dandy of a truck for me. I'm to come for Sunday Dinner immediately after I get done with my two weeks at school, and then she has a friend who wants to show me an apartment, at a reasonable cost, in the adjoining town.

I explain again that the school thing involves Vermont only once every six months, and that I'll have to be getting back to Colorado very soon after I'm done in here.

I get finished, and go try to explain to the Financial Aid Department that unless they can get their act together I'll have to stay.

This seems to cause confusion on their part. I explain patiently, to a whole chain of command, that I am a full-time student, and inherent in academic excellence is grocery shopping, book-buying and housing. This seems to cause confusion also. But as they have a week to go, I'm only terrified of it.

These people are an afflicting wound grievously borne by anybody who goes to school on the cheap, and all great ventures that rest on the backs of incompetent bureaucrats. I started with a traditional school "Office-Lady", and wound up talking to a Captain. Par for the course.

After that I go to lunch with several of my classmates, and a petition circulates, on a toilet paper roll, for the unceremonious disruption of the industrial Marriot Food Service bill of fare.

The consensus is: with a group that is roughly 30% vegetarian, grungeburgers and fat fried anything is an insult to anybody over the age of 16, and that Macaroni casserole and a salad consisting of one part tomato to five parts lettuce does not make a salad bar.

After lunch I explain my Financial Aid plight to a classmate as we sat cross-legged in a two hundred year old oak corridor near the Dean's Office.

I really believed, early the next morning, as I explained to the Dean of the College, The Dean of Students, two members of Campus Security, and a different Captain from the military portion of the college, that, as an American, and as an English Major (Which may out-rank a Military School Captain), that I was, by the Amendments of the Constitution, and the mission statement of the school, entitled, nay encouraged, to the free use of Metaphor and Hyperbole, and was, in point of fact, an avowed Rational Pacifist, with no actual intention of really, literally, "dynamiting the fucking Financial Aid Office".

161

They looked dubious.

I showed them Strunk and White.

They looked annoyed.

I showed them the Encyclopedia Britannica's section on style: they looked constipated.

I showed them the Bill of Rights in my wallet (You never know what somebody's going to do with one of those things!) and offered to let them search me, my dorm room, my class notes and the truck for dynamite. They showed me their teeth and told me it had better not happen again.

I asked if it had been metaphor, hyperbole, or freedom of speech that they objected to, and was called an asshole and told to get the fuck out of the office before somebody proverbially threw a literal book at me.

The thing is, I later discovered, that one of the Puritan ancestors of the Dean of the College had lost an argument, of sorts, with one of my Quaker ancestors (which is no trick) back in the late 1680's. His Ancestor ended up as the local boat inspector rather than Colonial Governor. His ancestor retaliated by having my ancestor jailed to death for religious heresy.

I should really be much more careful who I piss off.

Chapter 25

The Truck

"Just jump me some juice to my batt'ry...
Give that old starter a spin...."
- from Rusty Old American Dream, by David Wilcox

And then one day, like all the good things one ever finds, it was all over. Time to go home and do the work. Reading and Writing. Corresponding with my Mentor, beating my brain against the books. Financial Aid, eventually, kicked me enough to get home on, with the promise that the rest would be in the mail later in the week. Right.

The run downhill from Montpelier was fairly uneventful. Upon my return to the Old Man's treehouse, found another note leading me to the junkyard that had a cheap truck to get me back home.

The yard owned the semi tractor he drove for a living. Give my old man a black R-model Mack tractor with a sleeper and a decent radio, and he'll deliver anything anywhere. I phoned the yard and told them I was on my way.

My father, I assumed upon seeing the place, had led me astray. The place he worked out of looked like a vision of Santa's automotive workshop, if the Elves were on strike.

In the interest of not getting sued for libel I'll not describe the cast of characters, even in truth, but it would be fair to say that Carolyn Chute often describes the less colorful ones.

The junkyard office/shop was like a human roach motel. Giant tattooed rebel longhairs with beer cans permanently attached to one hand or the other, a guy who looked like all those people Buddy Hackett tries to look like, and at least one worn out barfly girlfriend. Some had been lured in by beer and companionship, others by racecars and the chance to use big hammers.

The bait for my Dad, of course, was that Mack tractor. Offer him one, and he'd push it around the world by hand.

The truck he had lined up for me squatted on three tires in a tangle of weeds by the way-back fence. There was a whole row of them back there: a '52 Chevy half-ton five-window that had been spit-polished and then using the industrial sized drum, Bondo'ed to within an inch of it's life. Then, probably some time after that whole sheet of front fender fell off, the revulsion and horror at the sacrilege had mounted, and the vehicle was used for target practice. Large caliber, lousy shot.

There was an Opel Kadet in similar shape: someone had beaten it to death with a pipe about an inch in diameter. You have to give the violent and stupid of the world some credit for learning at least one useful lesson from John D. MacDonald and old Cro-Magnon: Hit the soft places with your hand, for the hard parts, use a tool.

There was a fine specimen of the experimental Autobiologist's field in this area of the, ahem, field. The species Ford, genus Pinto, (to use the proper Binomial nomenclature) which some intent, and diligently busy, autovivisectionist had impaled with a long straight rod down though the windshield and floor pan, like a biology lab worm pinned to one of those wax bottomed pans. Thereafter removing most of the engine's secondary organs and tertiary support systems. No doubt for future dissection or emergency transplant.

David Wilcox's rusty old American Dreams were on their own, down there where the hill slopes off, in the land where even the faint of heart feared to tread. Right next to a little Land Rover, that could only be called formerly cute, and surely destined to die of culture shock, and the center section of a decapitated Lincoln Town Car, was the truck: The Truck.

The truck that I had phoned ahead and made reservations for. The truck that was currently six different colors and looked like something in a crayon portrait tacked to a grimy refrigerator by a young but psychotic chimp using a magnetic alphabet letter in a primary color. All mine. Consider me whelmed.

She had originally been a shade of baby blue, more or less, but somebody had undertaken to sand and primer the hood in black.

The fenders and part of the bed were a dark shade of red, chipped like the nail polish of a low rent whore, to reveal successive layers beneath, leading to a darker shade of blue.

"Observe, Dr. Watson, The truck was originally a light blue, and then repainted, no doubt for some nefarious purpose having to do with the world renowned automotive mastermind, Mr. Earl Scheib of greater Paintland, AND THEN, My Good Dr., it was painted this crimson red, so as, undoubtedly, to disguise it as a barn. Observe the chicken residue about the tailgate."

"Then", if I follow the trail of inductive reasoning, " continued Holmes, "and deductive logic, Doctor, someone had, in a fit of disgruntlement only possible with a sufficient quantity of discount alcohol, obtainable at those state run liquor stores which are so thoughtfully located near major highways and signs warning of the inherent dangers of their combination, realized that they were, in fact undertaking to restore a Chevrolet. The fiend then scratched the words *I want to be a Ford'* through the many layers of hood paint, turned the tail lights upside down so as to resemble said Henrian device, and crawled into that oversized moldering wooden box in the bed of the truck to die a broken man!"

"Utter Ruination!" the good doctor replies and continues.

"My god, Holmes! There is even a piece of the beast's rotting blue flannel among the oil soaked spare parts..."

HHmmm. Land Rover huh? Let's face it, my only knowledge about these things comes from a movie whose co-star was a Coke bottle. A chance to investigate.

Flat, bald spare tire bolted to the hood, mounts for a big air filter on the fender, just right for bush-bombing around in Kenya on the weekends. There was half a winch, which, if I could find the other half, I could use to suspend myself in Kenyan trees, should the lion not be sleeping tonight.

Maybe that would be worth a look. CREEEee-Thunk!

Somebody had taken the cylinder head off with a sledge hammer and the wiring harness looked like black spaghetti. In the process of opening the hood, I disturbed a bunch of field mice living in the number two cylinder. Interior? Ripped seats with exposed spiral springs, a deflated dog toy. Quite sorry to disturb you, Mrs. Mouse, can't stay to tea, good day. Clunkereeee-click.

Chevy Truck. Good Solid American Truck. "Like a Rock", says Mr. Seeger. What the hell kind of recommendation for a mode of transport is that? A rock is something that sits outside and nobody pays attention to it unless it's in the way.

It was what my old Cow Hampsha neighbor John Jerome used to call "your basic truck". His main criterion in bestowing this designation upon a vehicle was being a low weed- count underneath the vehicle, and a price not to exceed $200.

Take a look. Mud, oil slick, six flattened Cadillac hubcaps, and a rusted half pair of pliers and a piece of radiator hose under it. No plant life to speak of, not even poison ivy. Must be okay.

Interior: well, the doors don't match, and the seat is as ripped as a mummy's good Sunday shirt. What's this? AH haah!

Eureka! Foliage! Plant life. Fifteen inches of a pale, yet tenacious, sprout of Cannabis Sativa growing from a pile of dusty dirt down on the leeward side of the differential hump.

Cannabis Homis Chevroletis. No radio, but the plant life might give me something to do on the way home.

"Honest officer, it was just growin' there when I bought the truck."

We may have here a good argument for those little vacuum cleaners that plug into the cigarette lighter. Ooops, no cigarette lighter either. That explains it.

The cost of the basic truck has changed little over my lifetime. Two hundred is the flat rate for Truck, classification: physically present and theoretically willing to accept all the money you want to put into it.

These things are relative. Ya pays yer money and ya takes yer chances. You either pay the bank, or you pay the garage, and the physical state of any motor VE-hickle on the planet is said to be located somewhere in this economic axis (unless, of course, you buy anything vaguely resembling an A.M.C. Pacer, or [Thor help you], a Diesel Rabbit).

The other relevant vectors in the equation are, of course, the hobby versus transport axis, which shows just how many hours you are willing to waste on the bastard. So, rather than create a four dimensional representative graph of the quadlemma (quadlemma: twice the bull of a Dilemma), 'tis best to isolate the two groupings. It's much easier on the emotions.

There is an even simpler method for solving the complex equation of shitbox truck purchase. Two, in fact, depending on your situation:

1) Ask spouse or significant Other, who will have vectored the aforementioned equation to some tangential factor in your emotional development back about the time you started thinking how handy it would be to have a truck in your life, or,

166

2) Flip a coin, and abide by what it tells you on the first, best two out of three, or three out of five tosses: A coin toss is a simple way to access you subconscious, and the truck in question will abide your decision either way. (really)

3) Buy something new and reliable, shut up, and pay the nice man down at the bank: It'll save many late Sunday nights spent flat on your back with a droplight, skinned knuckles and those terribly haute couture motor oil hair treatments.

The solution here was easier, I needed a truck, or reasonable equivalent, to get home, and the cost of pick-ups in a town with (more or less) real cowboys, is somewhat inflated. In point of fact, the only people who really look like cowboys are the Indians (and Rubbermaid makes the best gun racks in the world, go figure). The cost of the truck would be equivalent to bus fare anyway, and the cost of an incautiously purchased plane ticket would be far more than the cost of truck plus gas to get it home.

A poor student type can often survive for long periods on the pizza provided at the moving jobs of friends who could win Oscars for hitting themselves on the side of the head when discussing the upcoming move, and feigning surprise as they say in faux-realization "Why that's right, you've got a truck....".

Since the purchase price included browsing privileges to the whole junkyard, and the damned thing was missing it's carburetor anyway, and a lot of spare parts could be stashed in that toolbox, it seemed reasonable.

The idea of your basic utilitarian truck is that parts for it are easily repairable, and failing that replaceable. It's ugly, but it's paid for, pays for itself (theoretically), and can be fixed with a rusty pair of pliers and a bent screwdriver (included).

$200? Ok, Ya got any paint?

It takes four days, when you count 'em all up, to build the basis of the truck. The tranny came from an Olds '88, a newer six cylinder motor with electronic (they used to be called "pointless") ignition from a Chevy Nova, radiator from a Buick that has seen better days and the power steering unit from a Pontiac that won't have any more days at all.

A radio is found, on the floor of a junked Volkswagen, and a small pile of carburetors, starters and alternators make it into all the nooks and crannies of the oversized toolbox. 1972 Chevy trucks don't have many more significant parts than that.

The paintjob, paid for in beer, is executed by a guy with four teeth in his mouth and little blue Vietnamese characters tattooed on his earlobes. It takes a couple of hours.

The paint is mixed out of the remains of a dozen old cans, and ends up the greenish color of an old tattoo. We literally cobble an exhaust system out of pipes from junked cars, and I've seen more structurally substantial lace.

Once this rickety old monster from the Delorian Age is able to rattle down the road it does, making the rounds of friends and family.

The guy who owns the junkyard, knowing from my dad that I used to ride motorcycles, gives me the rusted hulk of a Honda chopper that I'd have killed for back when I was about 18. But the joys of 18 are often the logistics problems of 26. I eventually end up giving it to Tony, who I haven't seen in a while.

He's delighted. He gives me a tape that we used to make fun of when they'd advertise it during old movies: two guys in longhair wigs carefully saying groovy like they want to mean it. They are hyping a tape of sixties and seventies music, and we had always found the ad hilarious. One of the women he dated after his divorce had given it to him for serious. He gives it to me the usual way: stuck to the back of the truck's sun visor with the word "asshole" written across a piece of duct-tape.

I visit my Grandmother, and, among other things hear that Sonny Barron, an old friend of the family, has enrolled his youngest in College this summer, and has locked himself in his basement to rebuild his old Harley.

The day before the last day back I go to visit with my Mother's sister, the last member of the family line on that side, aside from myself and her two kids. We have the Genealogy back to 1585, because we discuss genealogy when we can't discuss my mother anymore.

I envy her the fact that she married a good guy with a solid career, and that they seem so normal. Her kids are wonderful, and sometimes I wish I were sane enough to settle down and have some like that.

Most of the time I wish I could start over from where they are.

Chapter 26

Leaving

"I am,
alone
Sitting on a wall by the sea,
What a wondrous Ocean,
The waves call to me,
To join their fun,
To join their frolic,
The night is beautiful.
Darkness can be overwhelming
But not tonight.
Tonight the stars shine for me,
and the moon,
With all its illuminating light,
Shines for me.
With a hand for me
To join the dancing on the
ocean top
Am I alone?"

poem by Cathy Foster (10/23/47 to 1/29/75)
in the Malden High School "Lion", Fall 1964

The grand tour of friends and social obligations keeps the truck and I moving for almost a week. A week spent on couches after four A.M. conversations, and playing the catch-up game. A week of connections reaffirmed. A week of, not nostalgia, but living memories...

The carburetor gets repaired in Tony's driveway, the two of us leaning on the fenders. The electrical system gets taped and debugged at Judy's, with her sitting next to the truck in a folding chair. I rotate the tires, so the big ones are on the back and the smoother ones are on the front, while putting in a shift watching Jan's kids. Had a panicky moment when I thought the oldest had swallowed a lug nut.

There is a friend from grade school dying of A.I.D.S, alone, except for "staff", in a gothic ancestral Andover mansion.

A girl I knew from the High School Smoking Area is a Cop.

The first girl I ever kissed has kids now.

My best friend from seventh grade is doing time for B & E, Possession and Assault.

There is an ex-girlfriend of my father's, who was more of a parent to me than my Dad was, dying of Breast Cancer.

The first girl I ever talked about leaving town with runs a Sandwich Shoppe started by her grandfather.

The second and third girl I ever talked to about leaving are nowhere to be found.

Shit, the whole area is filled with the people, things and places I've loved. So many of them have been hurt or died. The smell of death is embedded in the shade of the old trees.

The suburbs of slow death by conformity, the musty old colleges where ideas go to die, the twisty back roads where young people die in cars, the house where my family died, our land covered with a shiny new house where strangers live, many years after the fire. History is death, and sometimes that's all right.

The place has History, just like you see on television. Yea, I'm from those famous places full of old memories: The factory towns of Lawrence and Lowell, where sweet young farm girls of the 1800's sold their youth to the machine. Salem, where they sell souvenirs of the Witch Trials.

As trite as it sounds, I can't go home again. Sure, I can visit the inordinate number of friends and relatives I still have in Eastern Massachusetts and southern New Hampshire, but I can never be at home there again. Not just yet.

Some nights I dream the tree lined roads of small Massachusetts towns, pothole for pothole, and tree for tree, but never again can it be home. Not just yet.

The night before departure, having left a note for my Father because he's still out working, I go to the beach. Barefoot, socks tucked into shoes, with my "trousers rolled" I wade the shallows at a beach my mother and I walked as a child. In a way we own it, she and

170

I. Before she died she would come here to think herself away from the world, and I always come here to miss her.

She died, along with my stepfather and three siblings, when I was nine years old. One of those tragedies you see on TV. My parents had been divorced five years at that point, and I went to live with my father.

In the West I am free of these things, but here I have to see it all. Relive it all.

I'm standing and watching the tide, knowing it only means what it means to me. Maybe it means the same to all people, everywhere, and we just agree not to talk about it, I don't know.

I feel like Federico Fellini in the opening from the movie "8 ½". Tethered. Floating high above the beach. Afraid to crash back down. Crashing back down.

Everyone goes to the ocean for clichés.

The ocean is the only place with a horizon here, and it is a horizon that says you must make a preparation for the journey.

You must build yourself a boat, you must pack a lunch. The plains of the West are a little more forgiving, cleaner. Room to run.

It's funny. In Old Europe, going into the West was the metaphor for death.

The horizons of The Future, like those of the airplanes, will contain few places to rest between sanctuary. The sweetest word in any language: Sanctuary. Home, fulfillment, an end to the spastic thrashing about that is not death.

Fires on the beach are illegal here, and the motor is beginning to lope. I have no adequate way to say goodbye.

It is time for the road again....

I grew up here, on the tiny back roads and main streets that, just like the legends say, used to be cow paths. Three hundred years of my ancestors had been born, died, and returned to the soil here.

And then, one day I left.

Chapter 27

Songs of Time and Distance

"By the late 1930's, Adolf Hitler's capacious autobahns had sparked Americans' imaginations. The ability to drive long distances at high speeds intoxicated people, just as the notion of owning one's own motorized conveyance had at the turn of the century. In 1939, far and away the New York World's Fair was General Motor's Futurama. As six hundred people at a time rode through GM's mockup of America's future, recordings synchronized for each rider's chair told how someday soon everyone would be able to speed at 100 miles an hour on fourteen lane superhighways and how expressways would be routed strategically through cities, to bulldoze ugly slums and outmoded business districts."
- from Getting There: The Epic Struggle between Road and Rail in the American Century by Stephen B. Goddard

"Our culture is fucked. Joseph Campbell said that it was because we were in need of rituals. That our culture needs a sort of vision quest..."
- from foreword to the play "Twister", by Ken Kesey, Boulder, CO., July 4 1994

Sometimes, especially when I'm driving long distance alone, there's this place I go in my head, like everybody has. Traveling is how I access mine. Some days it's a cafe in Paris, a place I've never been, or a forest cabin in northern New England, where I have.

Sometimes, in these fantasies, I'm alone. Sometimes there are friends, or music, or conversation, or silence. Maybe these are dreams.

At their best and most interesting there are friends I've known, and friends I'd like to have known.

As I drive the rickety green pickup away from the place I used to call home, and I can see, as if projected on the inside of the windshield of my mind, my friend Eleanor, who used to be a Vietnam Medic and a surgical nurse.

She was intentionally homeless when I knew her, and I thought it sad, but she was not. She lived in a van that had firewood and blankets and gold dust panned from a Colorado river. Packed in among her survival gear she had sterile Med kits for births among the Rainbow Family, and a nursing certificate she kept current by selling the occasional intricate hand knitted sweater. I imagine her bringing chamomile tea to Psyche and Prozac to Ophelia. I've met children she has midwifed who have names like Rain and Orion.

The truck has a natural groove at fifty-two miles an hour. When needed it can be pushed to a wobbling and incontinent sixty three, but the oil consumption is high at that speed and visions of front tires rolling down the road ahead of me as I bounce over the guardrail dance in my head when I do this. I bought a radio speaker at a small-town yard sale for the princely sum of fifty cents, and the stereo refuses to give back the only cassette tape I have with me, so the only option is to disconnect the wires when I don't want music.

Home, if that's what that place was, drops away behind me as I push the creaky rattrap out the old Route 2, heading for the New York State border. The rolling hills or verdant trees make me more homesick than the house of my father. Does this make me a bad person?

Periodically I stop at places, like the high span over river and pines of French King Bridge, or the murderous Hairpin Turn. They occupy some obscure location in high memory.

Route 2 is the old Hippie Highway- before the Mass. Pike: before Hippies, really. Before Arlo Guthrie and James Taylor, there was Norman Rockwell, the Entire Boston Pops, and Charles Godwin's mail to Miss Emily.

I stretch my legs, smoke too many cigarettes and drink too much soda and coffee, standing around at these sacred sites as if waiting for that magical catalystic something to happen. It never does.

I walk the circle layout at the North Adams Cemetery, and circle the Danvers State Hospital. I've looked under the Golden Gate and the Brooklyn Bridges. I even looked under the bridge at Lexington and Concord, and I sit and wait for the show to begin, for the event to occur, for the one great sign that will bring meaning. In this place, at this time, it hardly ever does.

In Lowell I saw the memorial site for Saint Kerouac; a ring of waist-high granite pillars behind the Post Office. It was too dark to see

173

if they said "Kerouac slept here". I was hours late for the unveiling, and the crowds had left. In Boulder the crowds would have filled the streets. Jack probably would have been late, too.

There was only one guy there when I got there. Skinny older guy from Minnesota, playing Bob Dylan songs on a guitar. When he took a break from playing to warm his hands I talked with him. Two guys talking at a memorial, talking in the darkness, trying to figure out what life means. Neither of us knew, but we both agreed it was the best game going so far. He also told me I should quit smoking.

My mind, unbidden, reaches back and creates weird pastiches of what was and what will never be: I imagine Edward Abbey and old Papa Hemingway: bearded men with dark brown bottles of beer in their huge hands. I imagine them flipping burgers in the backyard with Coyote Jim, who was known in some places as Paco The Werewolf.

The Coyote worked nights in a Boulder 7-11 when I knew him, and would go sometimes to a secret cave he knew of up in the hills to obtain quartz crystals he traded to the Boulder New Agers for acid (and food before he got the job).

Paco was the one that first told me about the full moon drum frenzies on Mt. Shasta, and his own fondness for crawling around the desert fried to the eyeballs on acid and mescaline combos. He was last seen heading for Santa Cruz on a decrepit Yamaha motorcycle with five headlights on the front and a pet ferret tucked inside his shirt.

As I drag the ragged ass of the rust laced Chevy over the hills, bridges and rivers of Western Mass and Eastern Upstate New York (a world away from New York City) I imagine the Valhalla of all house parties, staged somewhere with a view like that from the old Rockefeller mansion down on the Hudson. My imagination calls up humans, living and dead, known and unknown.

Over there is Steve From Boston, with the ice cream cone apostrophe returned to the right side of his name, hanging out with those two gnomes from Vermont, making delirious ice cream and Kailua drinks in the kitchen with the ancient Osterizer.

I imagine, over at the computer, in a broad sun splashed library, Mr. Salinger, with the help of his Russian co-Vermonter, and some guy in John Lennon glasses preparing a lengthy Unfair Usage lawsuit against some lunatic with a gun and a tattered paperback. A

Japanese woman in a kimono and dark glasses makes tea on the woodstove.

Out in the garage my nimble imagination conjures a folk hero from the unlikely town of Lowell, Massachusetts, sitting in lumpy American lotus on the hood of a '47 Hudson. He's listening to a skinny guy in flapping chinos doing a speed rap on the metaphysical implications of the use of ancient and holy fossil fuels in privately owned motorcars and the saintly beneficent nature of drive-through restaurants, liquor stores and wedding chapels, while changing the oil in a day-glow school bus and pounding out John Bonham rhythms on the oil pan and suspension. Ahem.

A wise grey-bearded publisher tells them, every so often, to put it all down on paper, and a prissy little chap in a white suit, who nobody remembers inviting anyway, yaps like a small, inbred dog about how writing is better than typing. A cadaverous old man marveling at a pocket calculator takes aim and shuffles the manuscript that became the book you're reading right now like a tarot deck made of leaves. The skinny guy raps onward with his extrapolative narrative tale of highway theology, and the car top Buddha (who now claims that he's a hood ornament) takes a nap.

Sometimes as I drive I just imagine the thing that is called silence, but is really the sound of the wind and the birds nestling and nuzzling the pines. Do you know how it feels to be hypnotized by the sound of a rushing mountain creek? Do you know what a yellow cactus flower smells like at nine thousand feet above sea level on a May morning after the last dusting of snow? Do you know what it feels like to hold in your hands a thing, of wood or iron or clay that you have made with your own hands? You should.

My mind unbidden spends its time this way as the miles, towns and states tick by like pickets on a stick dragged fence. I dream waking a lot when traveling, because I'm often alone.

On this trip it is a way to keep from listening to the tape from Tony. When I want to plug into the real world I wrap the wires under the dash back together. When I get home, lacking tools presently, I promise myself that the first thing I am going to do is get that damned tape out of the deck. When I'm in a car alone I get tired of silence after a few hours. A few hours after that I manage to forget any music I've ever known and end up singing beer commercials to myself. For some reason this only happens in cars.

It takes five days this time, though I've done it in half that time, letting the tape cycle one side to the other, auto-reverse repeating like a twenty-seven minute mantra. The nights I spend mostly, playing gutterball between jersey barriers in those twenty-mile stretches of road repair one-lane down in Pennsylvania. The humidity of Ohio, with it's carefully constructed rest areas featuring specimens of all the state's deciduous trees and auto-flush toilets fail to hold my interest. Truck stop lamps that look like Elvis can't do it either. Been there, done that.

The real space begins to open up in Indiana, home of those rolling little hills with all their interesting little caves (a story for another time, from another trip). By the time I've hit the regularly corrugated rolls of Iowa I'm totally hypnotized and can't imagine anything but a different soundtrack.

In Omaha I stop in on the bookstore of a friend of a friend, just in time for the Saturday night scrabble game that is attended by a half dozen people. They use five boards and a ten volume Oxford English Dictionary, and consume enough coffee for a platoon. When I finally leave, I steal an old coat hanger and use the stiff wire to get the infernal tape out of the deck, so now all I have to do is find a good radio station.

This too, as all things pleasurable to the flesh and the mind, must pass. It is hard to pick up the rhythm and only here is the pull of that giant elastic pulling east toward home really felt. It's usually ten or twelve hours across Nebraska and down into Denver. I start it in full dark after leaving friends on the warehouse industrial streets of Omaha, where the people listen to farm reports and the Punkers have to try soooooo much harder. It takes me eleven just to make Julesburg, the border crossing, and finally breath the sigh of relief that exiting Nebraska evokes.

I have an Arrow street guide that didn't make this trip due to space requirements, and the fact that I knew my entire route. It is spiral bound, and was shiny new when I bought it; late in the afternoon of the day I got my first Driver's License.

Now it is covered in coffee stains and deeply worked-in star petroglyphs of cigarette ash. The pages that have Oklahoma, New Jersey, and Arkansas on them were ripped out and burned, or sailed as airplanes out the windows of various cars as the states were actually and finally exited. Nebraska has a special place in both my

176

mind and in my map case. I don't tear it out for the personal reason that it gets an actual amount of active hatred on my part, combined with a certain grudging respect for Carhenge, up in Alliance and that bookstore in Omaha.

The map book depiction of Nebraska has, scrawled in its western sector, in imitation Mercator script, the legend "Here there be dragons" on one of the little western state towns where I got stranded. And on the other towns in that same vicinity, where I've broken down, run out of money and gas, been threatened by people who do obscene things to livestock and people with long hair, there are little black ink skull and cross bones.

If you squint at those pages it looks like freckles. Lots of freckles. Macon Georgia used to have a reputation like this, but I've been to Georgia, and although it's poor down there, and I have to take a grievous amount of shit for being a Yankee, it wasn't too bad.

I'm sure that I'd feel different about it if I were not a big "white" guy who can switch aspects with a fair degree of ease, but then there are a lot of places in America that you still shouldn't go as a Traveler no matter what you look like. I hate that it matters, but I think it's a universal, or at least planet-wide, thing. At least at it's grossest level.

Travel is never safe, won't ever entirely be, even in these supposedly modern times. It won't be when we all drive Buck Rogers Plexiglas cars and eat food pills.

But if you can afford to stay above the whole mess in an upholstered fantasy, then you might as well watch it on television. If you have to see it at ground level then there are some places you rush to, some you are drawn to, and some you just don't go if you can help it.

I don't mind New York, but you couldn't induce me to live there at ground level. The West is so unthinkingly, unimaginably wide, empty yet filled, that it will unnerve an average tiny mortal.

To live, say the Zen Folks, is to move.

Chapter 28

Home

"...I haven't found one yet, but I still have this
overpowering urge to hide in a box. Maybe it will go
away, maybe I'll be all right. Maybe it will get worse.
It's hard to say."
- from A Box To Hide In by James Thurber

The truck managed to get me into the driveway in one piece. It
would need work, eventually, but the rest could wait until later. There
were thirty books on the seat that I would have to read for school
before I could pay much attention to my so-called life.

The first thing I did was to go inside and get my thirty-two
ounce framing hammer and release the atoms of the accursed tape.
Nothing personal Tony, but If I have to hear "Smoke On The Water"
right after "White Bird" again I cannot be responsible for my actions.

Maryanne followed me along to the back yard, made nervous
by my determined focus, commenting on what a nice truck it was and
how glad she was to see me and how sorry she was about the death of
my futon, etc..

In later research I came to understand that my futon's death
had occurred:

A.) Through no fault of her own.

B.) As a result of inevitable circumstances.

C .) She brought one of the cats, who urinated on the futon,
necessitating the lighting of incense, which caught fire to:

> 1 a. The futon, burning a circular hole in it four
> feet in diameter.

> 1 b. The futon and the tent, effectively plastic
> wrapping it.

1 c. The futon, the tent, and the surrounding X number of feet/acres of forest; necessitating:

> 1 c-1. The national guard and the forest service, complete with smokejumpers and slurry bombers.

> 1 c-2. A conveniently located fire. Extinguisher.

> 1 c-3. A bucket or canteen of water after it had mostly burned itself out.

D.) Because her camping compatriots were:

> 1 a. Tripping on controlled substances.

> 1 b. Hexing her

> 1 c. Trying to kill her as part of an offering to Baal, the Fire God. (Note: to the best of my knowledge there are no really devout followers of Baal in Denver - I checked around, just in case.)

> 1 d. Trying to save her life.

> 1 e. Asleep.

E.) Because Maryanne was having a weird cycle on her lithium or just her cycle.

F.) Because Maryanne screwed up, burned the tent down and lied to cover it up and forgot who she told what.

G.) An act of God or Gods conspired to fuck up Maryanne's day.

H.) Shit happens.

I.) Shit happens often to Maryanne.

J.) As the result of some sort of Vengeance being dealt by someone known only to the roommates.

The house was the same. The street had been cleaned recently. The neighbors on the north, who had had a farm down in Mexico, but never had a lawn before, kept watering the painted brickwork on the side of our house.

The wall lay puddled on the floor....

Though it refused to grow, it had shed its internal plaster in preparation for the day that it would.

A black widow Spider that had taken up residence in the corner of my bedroom above the desk, way back before I had moved in, had swaddled up some more flies like so many captured hobbits.

Sometimes I think of those pictures from the Sixties research projects and contemplate feeding her hallucinogens. Sometimes, I'm sure, she wonders if she has enough thread in her belly to wrap me up. She and I, we have an agreement about it and keep our respective distances.

I took off my shoes, my poor baked feet breathing free for the first time in seeming months. The sole of the right shoe still bears the slightly melted mark of the edge of the floorboards of the truck.

I walked around the outside of the house, padding the dust of its baked hardpan front yard, and clucking to myself about the deforestation of the now knee-high weeds out in the back, wondering if I'd find any tennis balls or useable car-parts in the aftermath.

I mow the lawn, for some reason related to exhaustion, after a fashion, using an old oak-framed push mower, and get the cap of an old beer-bottle imbedded in my right arch. I don't notice the circular impressions until I'm done and back inside the house. The peroxide foams for several minutes, and I realize that it sort of hurts.

Pain is the body's way of saying stop: or learn to deal with a whole new thing. I decided to stop. Having little perforated circles cut into my feet did not seem like a lot of fun.

The sheets I'd hidden in the desk drawer to keep Maryanne and the, now finally departed, beau from using all of them were there. The bed was gone, but that didn't really matter. It was my floor, and it was welcome.

All right gang, that's a rap. Thanks for coming along for the ride.

The coffeepot is no longer hot, and I'm damned tired.

Maybe if I get some money for this book I can finally get that long dreamt of mountain cabin. Maybe I'll travel a bit. Get a fast computer, a house of my own, and a woodstove.

What more could anybody ever want (other than a flame-proof futon)?

Fin

More Stuff

I include this correspondence With Dr. Kent Casper of C.U. Denver to illustrate my early thinking on directions while the work was in process the last time. 13 November 2002 - jd

7-23-94
From:
Joe Dellea
AKA: John Joseph Dellea, IV

Dr. Casper,

A couple of details first:

Could I get a copy back from you of those essays by M. Van Tubergen on the early genesis of sci-fi? I mistakenly gave you the only copies of them that I had, And Martha is a bit miffed at me presently, so I dare not attempt to get reprints from her.

I enclose an article about Armed Services Radio, Berlin (AFN Berlin) going off the air. Cultural milestone?

Okay, down to business:

The current draft of <u>Walking to Vermont</u> looks like it will top out at a shade over fifty thousand words. As a working title, I think it's all right, but I'm not sure in the long run. I'll worry about that as it gets closer to publication. (One must dream.)

According to Raymond Mungo's Learning Annex Guide to Getting Successfully Published (another awkward title!), that ought to be a bit over 200 pages of book. Do you remember Ray Mungo (Famous Long Ago Return To Sender, Life On Total Loss Farm, and a founder of Liberation News Service (later known as Campus News Service)?

Shape, form, and content notes:

Of course the whole thing is as derivative as a regional dialect, but the idea is to open up, in seemingly straightforward narrative opinion, the world of philosophical thoughts. I can only hope to be able to translate the thing into a patois that readers can comprehend.

The cynical can say that the The Lion King was written by Shakespeare, and that no original piece of humor has been done since Robert Benchley, but that is not quite the point. To quote a quip that Joseph Campbell made, "There aren't any original stories, only re-tellings with different window dressing".

The telling of the tale, genus Road Novel, has thematic derivatives that go back to before Homer. The point is the cultural window dressing and the commonality of perception that the reader feels with the narrative voice. An acerbic, or even acidic point of view is a great zone of safety because disgruntlement is an essential part of human perception. If we did not have this desire for change fire would never have been harnessed, the wheel would not have been created, and we'd still be eating whatever we could chase off the cliff with a spear.

That beginning is a pain in the neck, and I've been wondering just where you start a first-person dialogic road novel.

Kerouac starts it off with Sal Paradise receiving a letter from our beloved protagonist Dean Moriarty. Thus, in true Buddhist form, removing self from center.

William Least Heat Moon (AKA Bill Trogdon) begins Blue Highways by laying in bed, contemplating natural and environmental sounds, and the fact that he feels trapped by his surroundings, possessions and recent divorce.

John Steinbeck uses external weather as a catalyst for movement in both Grapes of Wrath, and (perhaps following a significant theme) Travels with Charley. This can be seen as a way of pointing up the interrelation between mankind and his surroundings, and can be stretched to the most mythopoetic extremes of archetypal trials, errors and eventual rites of passage that it would be best if I spared that rap for another time. Besides, Joseph Campbell did it better than I ever will.

Cervantes, who gave the form of the novel so many other themes, gives us Don Quixote, If I may throw this in under the rubric of Travel/Adventure, being a social outcast in his town, and needing to find resolution. With Quixote, by the way, the reader is painfully aware of the pitfalls and may easily assume an immediate and comfortable distance through sophistication. He is obviously a bit simple and sophomoric, as emphasized by the unwise choice of a yellow swaybacked horse and out of fashion armor. Cervantes uses this to great advantage by causing the reader to underestimate Quixote.

Herein lies one of the may themes that I'm trying to weave into this basket(case) of a story: the wisdom is in the details and under-examined assumptions. The cliches that I'm trying to weave in are supposed to look simple. I'm working on tightening the basket's weave so they don't seem as apparent, but I think that some of them need to be a bit clumsy.

Architectonically:

I think that the structure of combined narratives tends to be the way to go with this thing. An interspersal of "present" with "past" and imagination, as well as periodic rants, outbursts and musings will work to bring out the "instant Gestalt" method of interpretation. This is not as Hardcore Punk as it sounds, nor is it an unusual structure. Joyce used it to convey the gestalt of an entire day, and in more non-linear recent writers it has been bend around a single focus of some sort. Amy Tan, and many of the eighties writers used it to point to an un-materialized center in their works that was usually a quest for self. My own awareness of the non-linear method comes from Margaret Atwood's Cat's Eye, which uses the same kind of structure that I am trying to build here. The main protagonist is seen at a key point in her life, which is, of course based on all the smaller preceding events in her life, and consequently account for an action that would make little sense out of the full context. It is a tough form.

Myself, I contemplate doing the whole thing under an assumed name and killing the narrative voice off in a frame story sort of ending that assures the whole "Marked for death" cachet that our culture loves so dearly. (Tremendous aftermarket for the undiscovered, previously unpublished stories of...)

What I'm trying for, I think:

Part of this is that there is, as I said, a certain commonality of experience in human perception, a shared awareness of pain and disillusionment. This may be a fairly depressing book.

End of correspondence with Dr. Kent Casper

History is a collection of the interaction of lives. Lives are a compilation of vectors, trajectories and actions. If a thing occurs differently, all the things that would have affected that thing are in different places.

My family died in a freak accident in 1975. They never saw Star Wars, the rise and fall of Disco, the end of Vietnam War, the resignation of Nixon, smoke detectors, air bags in cars, mothers against drunk driving, the Reagan administration, home computers, microwave ovens, Rap Music, AIDS or cable television.

Take that vector away and my life would have been significantly different. Alter just a little and it could have been slightly different.

It's that way for everybody. Each moment is a choice, an action. Even an inaction is an action. Every moment could change a domino chain of events down the road somewhere.

In every moment you have the possibility of being patient zero. Ten dollars of the right resource, safely stowed for your descendants, spiritual or physical, could blossom into enough to make them wealthy in their time. A chance inhalation of building insulation as a child can put you in an oxygen tent for your declining years.

Every action must be done with deep awareness of future implications. Think it through. Make a habit of it.

In the Hebrew tradition there are seven or so levels of good deeds. Mitzvahs, ranging from doing something you are obligated to do, but do not enjoy, for someone you don't like, to doing something that is easy for you that benefits you know not who. It's not a bad system if you think about it. Most cultures have some parallel.

In Japan they have a game called Pachinko. It used to be translated for Americans as "Japanese Pinball" It is played by scooping handfuls of approximately 3/8 inch ball bearings into the top of the game and the balls bounce through hitting dozens of pins and racking up a score. The trajectories involved are so complex as to fall into the realm of Chaos Theory. All interactions have an effect.

In some places in the north woods there are cabins & line shacks- built by whoever happens to be there, used by whoever happens to need it. It is the custom to have a blanket or two and some stored food in these places. If you need it, you will never forget it and never leave it unstocked. Being close to the edge should make you remember.

Yea, the next hitchhiker on the road might be a Manson wannabe, or it might be the Buddha, or it might be you or me.

If you are a Manson wannabe, do the world, all of us, a favor & chuck yourself off a bridge, take yourself out of the gene pool. If you are the Buddha, try not to mess with anybody too badly.

If it's you or me, hop on in.

John Joseph (Joe) Dellea IV
14 November 2002 - jd

Afterword by the Editor

This is the only discovered book of John Joseph "Joe" Dellea IV. Joe was my best friend for the past nineteen years and he suddenly passed away last December. I hadn't realized how much I had relied on him until he was gone.

Of course he edited my work, critiquing what didn't seem plausible. It wasn't a speedy process, but the cost was good; basically free.

I have battled depression for over three decades. Joe was an apt listener and often had extremely helpful insights on how to cope with my inner demons. Over the years, he probably saved me thousands in shrink fees and my life on at least one occasion.

One part of the profound loss I felt was that Joe never lived to see his book in print. We had talked about it, but his move to Fort Lupton derailed that endeavor. Unfortunately, he passed before we could get it edited and published.

When Joe was alive, our intent was to publish his book as non-fiction (despite it's subtitle) with my publisher. I was all set to format it and work on cover art with him, but he wanted to do a final edit, since he hadn't looked at it when he gave me a copy back in 2002.

After he passed, I was fortunate enough to obtain a very clean digital copy of the draft he let me read in 2002. As one can tell from the letter Joe wrote to Dr. Casper, this 2002 draft was not what he envisioned for this work. There were several chapters that he had not yet assigned titles or he had not selected quotes for them.

A few chapters had notes for guidance, like at the beginning of Chapter 17 where Joe normally would have had a title and put a pithy quote relating to the chapter after it, providing insight into the chapter. Instead he wrote, "'Strange City' bit from the Wasteland or something from the Doors".

At the end of Chapter 4 he had three paragraphs, separate at the end, with this note;

"End of chapter 4- There are three paragraphs below that I want in this chapter, Faithful Readers. I'm too close to this story to see where they go- or if they are too over-the top preachy. I could use some advice... Joe".

I read through Chapter 4 and inserted those three paragraphs where I believed they related to the thoughts, ideas, or actions that preceded them. Often this segued into the following paragraph better than before the insertion. Where he gave me some instructions, I followed them the best that I could.

Other than those aforementioned editing tasks, I corrected the few typos I found and retrofitted the rare clunkier sentences so they rolled through the brain a little smoother. Whenever I was doing this, I always asked myself, Would Joe like this better than what he had?

If I could honestly say yes, I kept it. If what I wrote wasn't something he would write, I changed it back. After looking it over prior to writing this, I feel that I was able to communicate Joe's narrative without injecting too much of my style.

I think Joe would have liked how it came out. Parts made me laugh out loud; others communicated the poignancy of life as a human on this rock hurtling through the universe, others tapped the sorrow in my own heart as I read some of the difficulties Joe encountered on this trip. Throughout it all, he was able to communicate the commonality of the human experience in all its joys, fears, sorrow, loves, and passions.

And, I believe that, Dear Reader, was what Joe set out to do.

A. D. "Big Al" Patterson

CPSIA information can be obtained
at www.ICGtesting.com
Printed in the USA
LVHW090833101219
640003LV00004B/526/P